PIRATES

*"Any book without a mistake in it has had
too much money spent on it"*

Sir William Collins, publisher

Pirates

Iain Zaczec

ff&f

Pirates
Facts, Figures & Fun

Published by
Facts, Figures & Fun, an imprint of
AAPPL Artists' and Photographers' Press Ltd.
Church Farm House, Wisley, Surrey GU23 6QL
info@ffnf.co.uk www.ffnf.co.uk
info@aappl.com www.aappl.com

Sales and Distribution
UK and export: Turnaround Publisher Services Ltd.
orders@turnaround-uk.com
USA and Canada: Sterling Publishing Inc.
sales@sterlingpub.com
Australia & New Zealand: Peribo Pty.
michael.coffey@peribo.com.au
South Africa: Trinity Books. trinity@iafrica.com

A catalogue record for this book is available from the
British Library.

ISBN 13: 9781 904 332 671
ISBN 10: 1 904 332 676

Design (contents and cover): Malcolm Couch
mal.couch@blueyonder.co.uk

Printed in China by Imago Publishing
info@imago.co.uk

CONTENTS

INTRODUCTION

PIRATES HAVE BECOME the most glamorous villains in the criminal world. In books and films, they are portrayed as swashbuckling adventurers, renowned for their sword-play and their fancy costumes. For their victims, it was a different story. They viewed pirates as monsters in human form, motivated solely by greed and cruelty. In part, this gulf between fact and fiction reflects the diversity of the crime. Over the years, pirates came from different walks of life and had very different aims. They even went by a variety of names, to justify their particular slant on the crime.

The heyday of piracy coincided with the era of colonial expansion, when the European powers competed with each other to acquire new overseas possessions. In these circumstances, it was extremely useful to have pirates harassing the shipping of rival nations. In order to legitimise this activity, governments described these adventurers as 'privateers'. They were granted a licence, known as a 'letter of marque and reprisal', which autho-rised them to attack enemy vessels. By using 'private' ships in this way, governments were able to save them-selves the expense of maintaining a large navy.

The term 'buccaneer' has become virtually synonymous with pirate, although there was once a very clear distinc-

tion between the two. The original buccaneers were
settlers on the island of Hispaniola (now Haiti and the
Dominican Republic). Most were French, although they
were joined by fugitives and refugees from other nations.
They survived by hunting the wild pigs and cattle on the
island, taking their name from the *boucan* - the frame on
which they cured their meat. The buccaneers turned to
piracy, after the Spanish drove them from their homes.

Some pirates were motivated by religion, as well as
money. In the Mediterranean, pirates were often known
as corsairs, a name that derives from the French *corsaire*
(a 'courser' or 'rover'). The Barbary corsairs, who operated out of Muslim bases in north Africa, were particularly notorious. They waged a holy war against Christian
shipping, making slaves of their captives.

Several terms were adopted from other languages. The
Dutch word *vrijbuiter* was translated as 'freebooter',
conveying the idea of 'one who roves about freely, in
search of booty'. The French form of this was *flibustier*,
which became anglicised as 'filibuster'. After the pirate
era, this took on a new meaning, describing a politician
who uses delaying tactics to disrupt the legislative
process.

Pirates themselves preferred more euphemistic terms,
such as a sea-dog or, in Holland, a sea-beggar. They also
described themselves as rovers. This could refer to a
wanderer or adventurer, although there are also overtones
of the Dutch word *rooven* ('to rob'). The most romantic
term was coined by the buccaneers, who styled themselves as 'the Brethren of the Coast'.

Pirates from Around the World

PIRACY HAS BEEN A PROBLEM, ever since maritime trade began. The term comes from a Greek word *peiran*, meaning 'to attempt' or 'attack'. In the ancient world, some of the Greek city states used to hire pirates to fight their naval battles, as they could not afford to maintain a permanent fleet - a measure that was echoed centuries later with the privateers. The Thracians, in particular, gained a reputation for piracy, especially around their favourite haunts on the island of Lemnos. The Greeks may also have devised some of the punishments that were commonly inflicted on pirates. They are said to have initiated the practice of keel-hauling (hauling a seaman underneath a ship). Similarly, the Carthaginians used to execute Greek pirates by binding a living man to a corpse and then casting them both overboard. In later years, the British navy also adopted this punishment for a time.

The Romans suffered the same maritime problems as the Greeks, coining the term *pirata* (taken from *peiran*), to define this activity. In their case, the main culprits came from Cilicia, on the southern shores of Asia Minor. From the 2nd century BC, Cilician marauders were so prevalent that they posed a threat to the economy of Rome itself. In response, Cilicia was turned into a Roman province in 102 BC, though the problem was not really solved until the reign of Pompey. In 67 BC, he was granted special powers, to clear the Mediterranean of pirates. His ruthless campaign led to the death of more than 10,000 pirates and the destruction of 1,300 ships. In addition, Pompey captured around 20,000 prisoners, forcing them to become settlers in farming colonies.

In the early days of piracy, raiders were often more interested in a ship's passengers than its cargo. Wealthy or influential travellers were always liable to be held for ransom. One of the most celebrated victims was Julius Caesar, who was taken captive in 78 BC, while journeying to Rhodes. He was then held for six weeks on the island of Pharmacusa, until the ransom was paid. During this time, Caesar warned his captors that he would return to punish them. He was as good as his word. After his release, he tracked the pirates down and had them crucified.

Many of the pirates' victims were not rich enough to merit a ransom. They faced a far bleaker future, as they were likely to be sold off as slaves. One of the many thousands to suffer this fate was St. Patrick. He was raised in *Bannavem Taburniae*, an unidentified location in western Britain. Then, at the age of 16, he was carried off by pirates and sold to an Irish chieftain called Milchú. Patrick remained with him for six years, tending his pigs and sheep.

The threat of slavery loomed large over travellers throughout the heyday of piracy. It was a particular problem in the Mediterranean, where the Barbary corsairs plied their trade, attacking Christian ships. They operated out of the three North African regencies of Algiers,

Royal Navy man-of-war attacking Barbary pirates

Tripoli, and Tunis, which were controlled by the Turks. They also had an important base at Sallee (now part of the city of Rabat, in Morocco). Many of the corsairs here were descendants of the Moors, who had been forced out of Spain and were especially keen to target Spanish shipping.

Prior to the 17th century, the corsairs generally relied on galleys, rather than sailing ships. Larger vessels often required as many as 250 Christian slaves to man the oars, as well as a number of free Muslim rowers, who might also assist in the fighting. In the main, however, attacks were carried out by janissaries (Muslim warriors), who took little or no part in the running of the vessel. Until the 17th century most of the galleys were state-owned, while the corsairs themselves bore commissions from their governments - echoing the practice of the privateers in Europe. Gradually, the number of private owners increased, particularly after 1627, when the inhabitants of Sallee rebelled against the emperor of Morocco and established an independent corsair republic.

The Barbary corsairs were a menace from the time of the Crusades until 1816, when a combined task force of British and Dutch ships destroyed the port of Algiers. In response to this threat, the military orders of the Church organised Christian corsairs, to plunder Muslim shipping. These included such groups as the Knights of St. Stephen, based in the Italian port of Leghorn, though the most famous by far was the Order of the Knights of St. John, which was stationed in Malta. These Maltese corsairs operated in a virtually identical manner to their Barbary counterparts. Like them, they held official licences, which gave them an air of legitimacy, and like them, they regarded themselves as privateers and their opponents as criminals. As was so often the case, piracy was in the eye of the beholder.

Pirates travelled far beyond the Barbary coast of Africa. They harried slave ships off the Guinea coast and rounded the Cape of Good Hope, in order to plunder traders in the Indian Ocean. In doing so, they often made use of the pirate bases on Madagascar. Discovered by the Portuguese in 1506, this island was initially used as a staging post for the Indies, but by the late 17th century, it had become a notorious pirate haunt.

The initial base was established by Adam Baldridge in 1691. A former buccaneer, he had been forced to flee from Jamaica after killing a man, taking shelter on the tiny island of St. Mary's, off the north-east coast of Madagascar. Using his pirate guiles, Baldridge soon became the unofficial ruler of the area, holding a personal court to settle disputes between local tribes. More importantly, from his point of view, he amassed a fortune by trading with his fellow pirates, exchanging food, ammunition, and other provisions in return for their stolen goods. Baldridge's profits were enormous. He could buy a pipe of wine (about 120 gallons) from America at £19 and sell it on St. Mary's for £300.

Not surprisingly, he was soon joined by other adventurers. In 1696, Abraham Samuel founded another pirate colony in an abandoned French settlement, in southern Madagascar. Like Baldridge, he lived the life of a potentate, styling himself 'King Samuel'. Both men were eventually overshadowed, however, by John Plantain, the so-called 'King of Ranter Bay'. Born in Jamaica from English stock, he had operated as a pirate in the Red Sea area, in a sloop called the *Terrible*, before arriving in Madagascar in 1720. Plantain was more ambitious than his predecessors. He built a stockade for himself and his followers, aiming to become ruler of the entire island.

For most pirates, the attractions of Madagascar were very similar to those on the islands of the Caribbean. Women and alcohol were in plentiful supply - both Samuel and Plantain kept 'harems' of the local girls - and there was no interference from the authorities. They could relax, repair their ships, and enjoy their ill-gotten gains at leisure.

There is no doubt that the Indian Ocean and the Red Sea offered rich pickings for pirates, but the opportunities were even greater elsewhere. With its growing empire in the New World, Spain had become a world superpower by the mid-16th century. It tried to consolidate its position through the Treaty of Tordesillas (1494), in which a compliant pope divided the rights to the world outside Europe between Spain and Portugal. Not surprisingly, the other European nations objected to this and began to harry Spanish shipping, while also attempting to build up empires of their own.

The first attacks came from French corsairs. In 1523, Jean Fleury captured two Spanish caravels off the Portuguese coast and was amazed to find that they were laden with Aztec gold and pearls. As news of these riches began to circulate, the French king actively encouraged other privateers to follow Fleury's example. The most renowned of these was François le Clerc, dubbed *Pie de Palo* or 'Peg Leg' by the Spanish, on account of his wooden leg. He captured a succession of merchant ships near Puerto Rico and Hispaniola and, in 1554, launched a successful raid on the principal Spanish stronghold on Cuba.

In due course, the French were followed by the Dutch and the English. The era of the 'sea dogs' was ushered in by John Hawkins, who embarked on the first of his four trading expeditions in 1562. It proved so profitable that his future voyages were backed by Queen Elizabeth, the Admiralty, and a syndicate of merchants from the City of London. On his third voyage (1567), Hawkins was accompanied by his young cousin, Francis Drake, who would soon overshadow his achievements.

The high point of Drake's career was his voyage round the world in the *Golden Hind* (1577-80), during which he ruthlessly plundered Spanish shipping. His richest prize was the *Cacafuego*, a Manila galleon which, according to a contemporary report, contained 'thirteen chests full of *reales* of plate [silver coins], four score pound weight of gold, and six and twenty tons of [uncoined] silver'. The success of this venture prompted other Englishmen to become privateers. Some were highly profitable, but many others bankrupted themselves in the process. Edward Glenham of Benhall, for example, sold his country estate, to fund a doomed attempt to capture an island in the Azores.

To the Spanish, of course, the privateers were nothing more than pirates and, indeed, the dividing line between the two was often very thin. There were some important distinctions, however, as the search for profit was combined with a fierce sense of patriotism and religious fervour. John Hawkins used to urge his men: 'Let every man serve God daily, love one another, preserve your victuals, beware fire, and keep good company'. The attitude of Blackbeard and his fellow pirates would be very different.

FAMOUS PIRATES

MANY OF THE STORIES about English pirates, whether true or fictional, stem ultimately from a single source - *A General History of the Robberies and Murders of the most notorious Pyrates* by Captain Charles Johnson. This impressive collection of pirate biographies was first published in 1724 and has gone through many subsequent editions. On the whole, it is accurate and well-researched, although some passages are clearly exaggerated or invented. In keeping with his subject, Johnson himself is a mysterious figure. Nothing is known about him for certain, although his obvious knowledge of maritime affairs lends weight to the theory that he was a genuine sea captain. For many years, it was thought that the real author was Daniel Defoe (1660-1731), writing under a pseudonym, but this idea has now been discarded. There have even been suggestions, based on nothing more than the authentic flavour of the book, that Johnson himself had once been a pirate.

Even if Defoe had no connection with Captain Johnson's book, he was certainly fascinated by the subject. On one occasion, he had a first-hand encounter with a band of Algerian pirates, during a trip to Holland. He also produced several publications on this theme - most notably his fictional account of *The Life, Adventures, and Pyracies of the famous Captain Singleton* (1720), which was loosely based on the career of Captain Avery - and, of

course, his most celebrated book is about a former privateer (*Robinson Crusoe*, see p.77).

For the earlier period, prior to the golden age of piracy,
the most important source is *The Buccaneers of America*
(1678) by Alexander Exquemelin. He travelled out to the
Caribbean as an indentured servant of the French West
India Company, arriving in Tortuga in 1666. Three years
later, he joined the buccaneers as a surgeon and shared
their lifestyle for more than a decade. It is clear that he
witnessed many of their raids, including Henry Morgan's
assault on Panama City (1671).

Exquemelin eventually settled in Holland, where he
wrote the *Buccaneers*. The book combined elements of
travel-writing - there are vivid descriptions of the flora
and fauna in the Caribbean - with graphic accounts of
torture and looting. It was published in several languages
and proved a huge, international success. This was due, in
part, to some judicious editing; in the Spanish version, for
example, Morgan was portrayed as a monster, while in
the Dutch and English editions he came across as a hero.

HENRY AVERY

For a brief period, Henry Avery (also known as Henry
Every or Long Ben Avery) was the most infamous of all
the pirates. Born in Plymouth in 1653, he worked as a
legitimate mariner for several years, employed by the
royal navy and by the owners of various merchant vessels.
For a time, he was also a slaver, operating off the Guinea
coast. Then in 1694, he signed up, along with several
companions, on a Bristol ship, the *Charles II*, which had
been chartered as a privateering vessel. Avery's aim was to
instigate a mutiny and seize the ship, a plan that was made
easier by the captain's fondness for rum punch. While he

lay befuddled in his bunk, Avery and his friends took over and persuaded the crew to turn pirate. Then, after renaming their ship the *Fancy*, they headed off to the Eastern Seas.

Using Madagascar as his base, Avery terrorised shipping in the Indian Ocean and along the Red Sea for the next 18 months, targeting many of the pilgrim vessels travelling to and from Mecca. Soon, he was in command of a small fleet of six ships, four of them from the American colonies. Their biggest haul came in September 1695, when they managed to intercept a flotilla of treasure ships bound for India. Avery immediately pursued one of the most impressive vessels, the *Ganj-i-Sawai*, which belonged to the Great Mogul. This appeared to be a daunting adversary, as it was armed with 62 guns and more than 400 musketeers. However, luck was on Avery's side. An early burst of cannon-fire brought down the Indian ship's mainmast, making it impossible to manoeuvre. Then one of its guns exploded, wreaking havoc on the deck. The remaining soldiers are said to have held the raiders off for a further two hours, but in the end it was the pirates' day.

The *Ganj-i-Sawai* proved to be a genuine treasure store. Avery's men made off with gold and silver worth around £50,000, scores of precious stones, as well as a saddle encrusted with rubies, which had been meant as a present for the Great Mogul himself. The total value of the prize was later estimated as at least £325,000. The pirates in Avery's fleet spent several leisurely days ransacking the ships they had captured. They also carried off a number of women, who were treated barbarously. After they had finished, the pirate ships sailed off to the island of Réunion, where they shared out the spoils. They then went their separate ways.

Avery took the *Fancy* to the Bahamas, where he bribed the governor to let them stay. In the meantime, however, the sacking of the *Ganj-i-Sawai* had caused an

international incident. The Great Mogul was understand-
ably furious and threatened reprisals against the East
India Company. Faced with this unpleasant situation, the
English government made determined efforts to find the
culprits. Eventually 24 men were arrested and brought to
trial. Six were hanged, while most of the others were sentenced to hard labour in the American colonies. Avery
himself was never caught and there is no firm evidence
about his ultimate fate. Captain Johnson relates that he
retired to Bideford in Devon, where he was swindled out
of his money and died in penury, 'not being worth as
much as would buy him a coffin'. Whether or not this is
true, Avery certainly became famous. A highly romanti-
cised version of his career became the subject of a play,
The Successful Pirate (1713), which enjoyed immense popularity, when it opened at London's Theatre Royal, in
Drury Lane.

—— WILLIAM KIDD (1645-1701) ——

All too often, there was a very thin dividing line between
pirate and privateer. The early part of Captain Kidd's
career was entirely respectable, winning the backing of
the British government, and it was only in his final years
that he fell foul of the law. Born in Scotland, the son of a
clergyman, Kidd became a legitimate sea captain, operating out of New York. During the wars against France, he
was engaged as a privateer, protecting English shipping in
the Caribbean.

Then in 1695, following Avery's spectacular coup, he
accepted a commission to hunt down pirates in the
Indian Ocean. Almost immediately, things began to go
wrong. Kidd had a run in with a navy vessel, which press-
ganged half his men, and he was obliged to replace these
with corsairs. When he arrived at his destination, the initial pickings were slim and Kidd's crew began to turn

mutinous. During one confrontation, he struck his gunner on the head with a bucket and killed him - a rash act
that would later lead to his downfall. In the meantime,
Kidd's men pressurised him into attacking a series of
smaller vessels, which brought little in the way of booty,
but which alerted both the East India Company and the
Whig government back home. Increasingly, it seemed to
them that the pirate-hunter had turned pirate.

Ironically, Kidd's most striking success - the capture
of the *Quedagh Merchant* in 1698 - fell more or less within the bounds of his commission. For, although the ship

was captained by an Englishman and the cargo was owned by an Armenian, the vessel was sailing with French papers. Kidd and his crew duly looted it, carrying off a rich haul of gold, jewels, silks, iron, and sugar. This wealthy prize was the basis of all the later stories about the pirate's hidden treasure.

Kidd returned to America in the following year, little realising that he was about to become a political scapegoat. In London, the government was being pilloried for its failed promises about suppressing piracy, so ministers decided to make an example of their former employee. Kidd was arrested in Boston, shipped back to London, and put on trial for piracy and for the murder of his gunner, William Moore.

The verdict was a foregone conclusion and, in May 1701, Kidd was sentenced to death. His fate was similar to that suffered by many other pirates. He was held in the notorious Newgate prison, before making his final journey to the gallows. The authorities were keen to deter other seamen for taking to piracy, so the sentence was carried out in plain view of shipping, at Execution Dock at Wapping. Crowds thronged to watch the spectacle, so it took two hours for the cart to make the three-mile journey from Newgate. Kidd passed the time in drinking as much rum as possible. When he eventually reached Wapping, observers noticed that he was thoroughly drunk. Even in this state, he must have been shocked when the rope snapped during his execution, and there was a ten-minute delay before he was hanged for a second time.

In keeping with Admiralty tradition, Kidd's body was tied to a post at the water's edge, until the tide had washed over it three times. It was then tarred and taken off to Tilbury, where it was put on display in an iron cage, 'to serve as a greater terror to all persons from committing the like crimes'.

Kidd rapidly became the focus of many legends. The most famous of these concerned his missing treasure (see p.28). However, balladeers also described how he buried the family Bible before taking to his life of crime, while others claimed to have seen his ghostly ship, gliding through the waters on days when there was no wind to power the sails. Some also talked of a travelling seafarer, his clothes dripping with water, who asked for shelter at lonely hostels and then promptly vanished.

JOHN GOW

John Gow was Scotland's most notorious pirate. In common with many of his kind, he started out as a professional seaman, before turning to crime. In 1724, he was appointed second mate and gunner on the *George Galley*, having previously served on men-of-war and a variety of merchant vessels. On the night of November 3, as the ship was heading towards the Straits of Gibraltar, there was a violent mutiny on board, instigated by Gow. The elderly captain, the first mate, the clerk, and the surgeon were all attacked in their beds. The clerk begged for a moment's respite to pray for his soul, but the only reply he received was: 'Damn you, this is no time to pray.' He was killed instantly and, like the other victims, his body was thrown over the side.

Gow was elected captain by the mutineers, who promptly forced the remainder of the crew to turn pirate. After renaming the ship the *Revenge*, they spent the next two months plundering trading vessels, along the coasts of Portugal and Spain. Then, as winter set in, they turned north, to take shelter in Scottish waters. By January 1725, they were safely ensconced in the Orkneys, which Gow knew from his youth. He went ashore to meet up with a former mistress while, in his absence, the discipline on board began to unravel. One of the forced men escaped from the *Revenge* and alerted the authorities. Soon, Gow and his men were fleeing for their lives, although this did not prevent them from stopping off at the tiny island of Cava, where they looted the home of the local sheriff and brutalised three women. They were arrested shortly afterwards, after grounding their ship on Calf Island. By March 1725, they had been transported down to London. Initially, Gow refused to plead, but he changed his mind after being threatened with the Press-Yard - a terrible place of torture in Newgate Prison, where uncooperative prisoners suffered a slow and agonising death, as a succession of heavy weights were placed on their body, gradually crushing them to death. He was subsequently hanged, along with nine members of his crew.

In many ways, Gow's career as a pirate was much more typical than those of his better-known peers. It was brief, violent, and entirely devoid of the boldness and enterprise that became such a feature of pirate films and books. Indeed, Gow's name would probably have been long forgotten, if he had not attracted the attention of two famous authors - Daniel Defoe and Sir Walter Scott (1771-1832). Defoe produced a racy pamphlet about the scoundrel, shortly after his execution (*An Account of the Conduct and Proceedings of the late John Gow, alias Smith, Captain of the late Pirates, executed for Murther and Piracy committed on board the George Galley*, 1725). Scott, meanwhile, used the story for the basis of his novel, *The Pirate*, which appeared in 1814. He played down the more brutal aspects of Gow's character, placing greater emphasis on the wild and romantic settings in the Orkneys. He visited many of these in person, travelling as a guest of the

Lighthouse Commissioners. By a curious coincidence, his chief helper was a lighthouse engineer called Robert Stevenson, the grandfather of the author of *Treasure Island*.

JEAN LAFITTE

The reputation of some pirates changed dramatically over the years, so that they are remembered as folk heroes rather than villains. Foremost among these are the Lafitte brothers, who were born in France in the early 1780s and arrived in New Orleans at the turn of the century. These were turbulent times in the area, as Spain returned its holdings in Louisiana to France in 1800, which in turn sold on the territory to the United States (the Louisiana Purchase, 1803). The competition between France and Spain offered considerable opportunities for both smugglers and pirates, and the Lafittes soon took full advantage of this.

Jean became the leader of a pirate community on Grand Terre Island, just off the Louisiana coast. In this disreputable spot, many seafarers set themselves up as privateers, accepting letters of marque to attack Spanish shipping and remove their cargoes of slaves and other goods. This proved such a menace to local trade that the pirate base was eventually closed down by the US authorities in 1814. In the following year, however, Lafitte did much to restore his reputation by assisting the authorities against the British, in the Battle of New Orleans. This dramatic turnaround transformed the pirate into a local hero - his life has been celebrated in books and films, and there is even a national park named after him. In reality, though, Lafitte did not abandon piracy; he simply moved his centre of operations further west, to Galveston in Texas.

WOMEN PIRATES

IN OCTOBER 1720, the career of Captain Jack Rackham was brought to an abrupt end, when he was caught unawares by a heavily armed privateer, who was hunting down pirates. A single broadside disabled Rackham's vessel and most of his men surrendered tamely. Only two of the pirates were prepared to fight, swearing profusely at their shipmates, in a vain attempt to rouse them. To the amazement of the arresting officers, it turned out that these were not men at all, but the notorious women pirates - Anne Bonny and Mary Read. Their story is remarkable, although the only source of information for their early lives is Captain Johnson's account, which may or may not be reliable.

ANNE BONNY

Anne was born in Ireland, the illegitimate daughter of a prominent lawyer, William Cormac, and his housemaid. The couple tried to avoid a scandal, by dressing the child in boy's clothes and passing it off as a relative's son. When this failed, the lovers fled to America, where William gave up the law and became a successful plantation owner.

Now settled in Charleston, South Carolina, Anne grew into a wild and troublesome young woman, who was always getting into fights. She also developed a taste for danger, often dressing up as a man and frequenting the taverns on the waterfront. During one of these episodes, she hooked up with a shiftless sailor called John Bonny. To her father's horror, Anne decided to marry him. When Cormac forbade this, the pair moved away to New Providence in the Bahamas.

Anne's relationship with Bonny did not last long, but she soon teamed up with an even more disreputable character - Captain Rackham, widely known as 'Calico Jack'. Through his association with Bonny and Read, he became a notorious figure, although in reality he was a small-time pirate. He learned his trade under Charles Vane, serving as his quartermaster on the *Independence*. He eventually took over this vessel in 1718, when the captain declined to attack a French man-of-war and was ousted by his mutinous crew. Rackham overpowered a number of fishing boats and small trading vessels, but never managed to capture a major prize. As times grew hard, he decided to retire and claim the king's pardon, and it was for this reason that he had come to New Providence. But, like so many other pirates, Rackham could not stay out of trouble for long. Together with Anne, he stole a sloop from the harbour and she embarked on her life of crime.

MARY READ

By a remarkable coincidence, Bonny was soon joined by another female pirate - Mary Read. According to Johnson, her early life was every bit as remarkable as Anne's. She was born in England and, like Anne, was the product of a broken home. Her mother was abandoned by her husband, who left her with a baby son. After his departure, she had an affair and gave birth to a second child - Mary. At around this time her infant son died, so Read decided to conceal her daughter's illegitimacy by passing her off as the boy. Mary, like Bonny, grew up wearing male clothing. She continued with this deception until her adolescence when, still masquerading as a man, she began looking for employment.

She took on a job as a footman but, finding this too dull, enlisted in the army instead, serving with a regiment in Flanders. There, she fell in love with one of her fellow soldiers, a Dutchman. They married, left the army, and set up a tavern in Breda called *The Three Horseshoes*. For a time, Mary's existence followed a conventional path, until her husband died suddenly from a fever and she was left on her own again. She soon returned to her former ways, donning male attire and signing up as a sailor on a Dutch ship, headed for the Caribbean. As luck would have it, this ship was taken by Rackham, and Mary was persuaded to join his crew.

The activities of Read and Bonny are well documented, from the time that they came on board together. Witnesses at their trial confirmed that they only disguised themselves as men during periods of combat: 'when they saw any vessel, gave chase, or attacked, they wore men's clothes; and at other times, they wore women's clothes'. The pirates' victims also confirmed that they were every bit as fierce as their male counterparts: 'they were both very profligate, cursing and swearing much, and very ready and willing to do anything on board'.

Rackham and his crew were tried in Jamaica, in November 1720. The men were tried separately and were all sentenced to hang. Anne visited Jack in his cell, but brought him little comfort. Instead, she accused him of cowardice, saying 'if you had fought like a man, you need not have died like a dog'. Rackham was hanged the next day and, as was the custom, his body was displayed in an iron cage at Deadman's Cay (now Rackham's Cay).

It seemed that a similar fate would soon await Bonny and Read. They were tried together and both were found guilty. At this point, however, they revealed that they were

Anne Bonny and Mary Read

pregnant. Once this was confirmed, the death penalty was rescinded and the two women remained in prison. For Mary this was only a temporary reprieve, as she contracted a fever and died in jail, in April 1721. The fate of Bonny is unknown, although there are claims that her wealthy father used his influence to secure her release.

Read and Bonny are the only female pirates who have been firmly identified from the golden age of piracy, but they were not the only women to become involved in such crimes. In Ireland, the exploits of Gráinne Mhaol (c.1530-1603), often anglicised as Grace O'Malley, were legendary. Born in Connaught, she was the daughter of a powerful chieftain, who maintained a sizeable fleet of ships, which were used for fishing and trading, as well as piracy.

From her base at Rockfleet Castle, Grace organised raids against passing merchant ships, as well as her political rivals. One of the latter described her as 'a great spoiler, and chief commander and director of thieves and murderers at sea'. In spite of this, she maintained the strength and reputation of the O'Malley fleet, even when she reached old age, and was granted an audience with Queen Elizabeth in Greenwich Palace.

Grace's exploits were echoed in China by Cheng I Sao. In the early nineteenth century, she married a pirate leader and joined him in terrorising anyone who sailed near Canton or the Pearl River delta. After her husband's death, she assumed control and expanded the fleet, until it consisted of more than 200 junks and other vessels. For three years, Cheng I Sao wreaked havoc along the South China coast, until the authorities called in Portuguese and British warships. Deeming it prudent to retire, she accepted a pardon in 1810 and later ran a gambling house in Canton. She never returned to piracy and, by the time of her death in 1844, had become a very wealthy woman.

Although there are few other documented examples of female piracy, it was not unheard of for women to disguise themselves as men, in order to join the navy. Mary Anne Talbot, for example, served on *The Crown* in the 1790s and was present at the British capture of Valenciennes in 1793. She left the navy after being wounded by grapeshot, and became an actress on the stage at Drury Lane. She was later employed by a publisher, R.S. Kirby, who produced an account of her colourful career (*The Intrepid Female or Surprising Life and Adventures of Mary Anne Talbot*, 1804).

Pirates
in the Caribbean

THE HEYDAY OF PIRACY in the Caribbean can be traced back to the arrival of the buccaneers. Originally, these were a community of settlers, who gathered, over the years, on the island of Hispaniola. They came from very diverse backgrounds. There were deserters, castaways, maroons, fugitives from justice, runaway slaves from the plantations, and political or religious refugees. There were different nationalities too, although most came from France, England, or Holland.

At first, the settlers lived as huntsmen and traders. They hunted the wild beasts on the island and, in the process, became expert marksmen, using a distinctive type of long-barrelled musket. They then bartered their meat, hides, and tallow, in return for guns, ammunition, cloth, and rum. The lifestyle of these buccaneers was undoubtedly pretty rough. They loved gambling and drinking - their favourite tipple was a lethal mixture of rum and gunpowder - but, most of all, they enjoyed their anonymity. No one asked any questions about their former existence. Essentially, they were harmless, but the Spanish authorities classed them as undesirables and were determined to root them out. They succeeded in this, although the buccaneers did not go very far. In around 1630, they moved to the island of Tortuga ('Turtle Island'), situated just two miles off the coast of Hispaniola. Inevitably, the Spanish tried to dislodge them from here as well, but this plan soon backfired on them.

Realising that they would have to defend themselves, the buccaneers banded together and began to attack Spanish shipping. As a token of their newfound unity, they called themselves 'the Brethren of the Coast'. These attacks were very limited at first, as they only had *piraguas* (large canoes), but with their lethal marksmanship, they soon managed to steal more powerful vessels. These successes, in turn, brought them new recruits and strengthened the buccaneers' resolve to make Tortuga their permanent home. This was made possible by Jean le Vasseur, one of their first leaders. He had been a military engineer, before his Huguenot beliefs forced him to flee from his homeland, and he put these skills to good use, creating a powerful stronghold around the main harbour on Tortuga. The growing reputation of the buccaneers attracted the attention of Spain's national rivals in Europe. Increasingly, they sought to commission them as privateers, to carry on the fight against their mutual enemy.

— Sir Henry Morgan (1635-88) —

Although most acts of piracy were carried out on the high seas, there are some instances of attacks being made on land-based targets, most notably those carried out by Henry Morgan. Hailing originally from Wales, he probably arrived in the West Indies as part of an expedition sent out by Oliver Cromwell in 1655. He would certainly have been an obvious choice, as his uncle was deputy governor of Jamaica.

Morgan soon joined the buccaneers in Tortuga, accepting letters of marque which gave him the authority to plunder Spanish shipping. As this became more scarce, he switched his attention to Spanish settlements, sacking no fewer than eighteen towns and cities. These included Portobello, Gibraltar, Maracaibo, and Chagre, but his

most impressive feat was the capture of Panama City in 1671. This entailed leading his forces through thick jungle, where they ran so short of food that they were obliged to eat leather bags, cutting them into strips and then softening them in boiling water.

In common with other privateers, Morgan's greatest danger came from the changing attitudes of his own government. After the Treaty of Madrid (1670), the hostilities between England and Spain were terminated, and the latter called for Morgan to be held accountable for his crimes. For a time, it seemed that this demand would be granted. In 1672, Morgan was recalled to England,

apparently to face the music. Instead, the authorities simply waited for the protests to die down, before rewarding
him with a knighthood and an appointment as lieutenant
governor of Jamaica.

In spite of these honours, Morgan remained a hated
figure in many quarters. He exerted little discipline over
his men, allowing them to commit numerous atrocities in
the towns that they looted. Drink was also a problem.
When he was in charge of the *Oxford*, his crew became so
drunk that they accidentally blew up the ship, while the
captain was busy dining with his officers. Similarly, after
the capture of Panama City, the treasure ship *La
Santissima Trinidad* was able to slip quietly out of port,
because Morgan's men were too drunk to prevent it.

FRANÇOIS L'OLLONAIS

Morgan's exploits were far from unique. The French
buccaneer, François L'Ollonais also took piracy onto dry
land, plundering the cities of Gibraltar and Maracaibo in
New Granada (now Venezuela). Nicknamed after his
birthplace (Les Sables d'Olonne, in Brittany),
L'Ollonnais arrived in the Caribbean as a servant but
soon joined up with the buccaneers. His greatest success
came in 1667, when he captured a Spanish treasure ship
carrying 40,000 pieces of eight and a rich collection of
jewellery.

Amongst the Spanish, though, his name became a
byword for cruelty. No other buccaneer took such delight
in torturing his victims. According to Exquemelin, he tore
out the tongues of any prisoners, who did not immediately reveal the location of their valuables, or sliced off their
limbs, a piece at a time. On one occasion, he terrified a
group of Spaniards by selecting a victim, cutting out his
heart, and then gnawing on it 'like a ravenous wolf'. As he
did this, he warned the others that 'I will treat you all alike

if you don't talk'. Fittingly, perhaps, L'Ollonais met a gruesome end himself, when he was captured by a tribe of native Americans. They tore him to shreds, threw his remains onto a fire, and then cast his ashes into the air, so that 'no trace or memory might remain of such an infamous, inhuman creature'.

By the start of the 18th century, a growing number of pirates were attracted to the West Indies, encouraged by the success of the buccaneers. They did not confine their activities to the Caribbean itself, operating along much of the eastern seaboard of the Americas. In most cases, however, they chose to make their base on one of the islands.

There were several reasons for this. First and foremost, they were safe. Most of the islands belonged to distant European powers, which were unable to police them effectively. This was especially true of the Bahamas, which had been claimed by England in 1670 and were inhabited by English settlers, but which were not formally recognised as a colony until 1718. The pirates took advantage of this power vacuum and flocked to the island of New Providence, which had a fine, sheltered harbour. Soon, this became renowned throughout the region as a safe haven for pirates, as notorious in its own way as Madagascar or Tortuga.

Pirates needed refuges of this kind, so that they could indulge in their favourite pastimes - drinking and womanising - without fear of arrest. More importantly, though, it gave them the opportunity to carry out repairs and adjustments to their ships, far away from the prying eyes of the authorities. In terms of maintenance, the most crucial task was 'careening' (from *carina*, the Latin word for 'keel'). This involved beaching the ship and then turning it over onto its side, so that the bottom could be scraped clean and coated with a mixture of wax, tallow, and tar. This process was vital, to ensure that the hull did not become overgrown with weeds and barnacles, which would affect both the speed and the steering of the vessel. Careening was a slow and laborious business, which left the pirates vulnerable to attack, so it had to be carried out in a secluded spot.

Pirates also required the same degree of privacy, when carrying out adjustments to their vessels. In the vast majority of cases, pirate captains acquired their ships by stealing them, so they were rarely fit for their criminal purpose. In the case of merchant ships, pirates usually removed the bulkheads - the internal, partition walls that were designed to protect the cargo. In addition, they were

NATIONALITY OF PIRATES OPERATING AROUND THE BAHAMAS, 1715-25

35 per cent **English**
25 per cent **American colonials**
20 per cent **Caribbean**
(*mostly Barbados, Jamaica, and the Bahamas*)
10 per cent **Scottish**
8 per cent **Welsh**
2 per cent **Other Europeans**
(*French, Dutch, Spanish, Portuguese, Swedish*)

always keen to add to their fire-power, which meant that new gun ports had to be cut. For obvious reasons, it was advisable to remain discreet about these changes.

SAM BELLAMY

One of the wealthiest prizes ever won by a pirate was the *Whydah*. In March 1717, Sam Bellamy and his men managed to capture this slave ship in the Bahamas, following a gruelling three-day chase. The *Whydah* was much larger than Bellamy's sloop and it was carrying a rich cargo of gold, silver, ivory, and spices. Gleefully, the pirate took both the ship and its treasure, though he did not enjoy his spoils for long. A month later, on April 26, the *Whydah* was caught in a terrible storm and sank off Cape Cod. Only two men survived, out of a crew of 146, and Bellamy was one of the casualties.

Bellamy's life has become the focus of a romantic legend. As a young sailor, it is said, he fell in love with Maria

Hallett, a girl from a wealthy family. Her parents were unimpressed by his prospects, so the lad went off to seek his fortune, looking for lost treasure in foreign ship- wrecks. When this failed, he turned to piracy. As 'Black Sam' Bellamy, he became the scourge of the Caribbean, looting more than fifty ships. With the capture of the *Whydah*, however, he was suddenly rich enough to aban- don these wicked ways. Renouncing his life as a pirate, he was sailing home to claim Maria, when he ran into the fatal storm.

Whether or not there is any truth in this tragic tale, Bellamy's career has certainly left behind one extraordi- nary legacy: the *Whydah* itself. Located in 1984, it has become the most celebrated of all pirate shipwrecks. Divers have retrieved thousands of artefacts from the remains, helping historians to build up a realistic picture of life on board a pirate ship. Many of the finds, including

COINAGE RETRIEVED FROM THE WHYDAH

Reales minted in Potosi, Nuevo Rieno,
Lima, and Mexico City
Escudos from Lima and Mexico City
Shillings, **Crowns** and **Half-Crowns**
from England
Centimes, **Silver Louis**, & **Sous** minted
in Paris, Limoges, La Rochelle, Bordeaux,
and St. Menhold
A **Bawbee** from Scotland

weapons, clothing, and jewellery, are on display at the nearby museum in Provincetown, Massachussetts.

Some of the most moving discoveries relate to John King, the youngest known pirate. He was just a child, when Bellamy captured the passenger ship that he was travelling on with his mother. Somehow, he persuaded the pirate captain to let him join their crew and, for almost a year, he took part in their adventures. Like Bellamy, however, he perished in the *Whydah*. In 1989, a child's fibula (leg bone), together with its sock and shoe, was recovered from the deep and, after tests at the Smithsonian Institute, it was confirmed that the bone came from a child aged between eight and eleven. This is thought to be John King.

In spite of the best efforts of the authorities, piracy in the Caribbean continued to flourish. One of the chief reasons for this was the vulnerability of shipping. Pirate vessels might often be smaller than their prey, but they were much stronger in terms of men and fire-power. In most cases, pirates used sloops, which were renowned for their speed and manoeuvrability, but they added extra guns, along with the crew to man them. On average, a merchant ship would be crewed by ten to twenty men, while a pirate ship would have upwards of eighty, heavily armed ruffians. Small wonder that most of the trading vessels surrendered without a fight.

Most pirate ships would, of course, have been no match for a fully armed warship. These were always in short supply, however, as the government in London usually had other priorities. In 1715, for example, there were just four English warships and two naval sloops patrolling the entire Caribbean. For much of the time, the royal navy was fully occupied with conflicts in other parts of the empire. Besides, many politicians still felt that pirates could have their uses, provided they confined their attacks

to enemy shipping, as in the days of the Elizabethan privateers. Even when these attitudes changed and there was a concerted attempt to rid the high seas of pirates, some colonial governors still bemoaned the lack of ships protecting their waters.

Not all governors shared this point of view. For many, the apparent apathy of the English authorities was a positive boon. Throughout the American colonies, there was widespread resentment at the economic restrictions imposed from London - under the terms of the Navigation Act (1696), the colonies were obliged to trade exclusively with England. This raised the price of imports considerably and, as a result, some governors were happy to do business with the pirates, buying their stolen goods at bargain prices. The most blatant case of this occurred in North Carolina, where the governor, Charles Eden, was content to offer shelter to Blackbeard, in return for a cut of his takings.

BLACKBEARD

The most notorious of all the pirates operating in the Caribbean was Blackbeard. He did not have the longest career, nor did he take the most ships or amass the greatest treasure, nor was he even the most violent of the pirates, but he had an unerring knack for getting under the skin of the authorities. His raids were spectacular and he had a positive gift for self-promotion, which earned him pride of place in the newspaper columns, on both sides of the Atlantic.

Blackbeard also ensured that he looked more fearsome than any other villain. Captain Johnson's memorable description of the pirate illustrates why so many of his victims thought that he resembled the devil incarnate. Johnson focused initially on his prodigious beard, which 'covered his whole face and frightened America more than any comet...This beard was black, which he suffered to grow of an extravagant length...it came up to his eyes. He was accustomed to twist it with ribbons, with small tails, after the manner of our wigs...In time of action, he wore a sling over his shoulders, with three brace of pistols hanging in holsters...and stuck lighted matches under his hat, which, appearing on each side of his face, his eyes naturally looking fierce and wild, made him [resemble]...a Fury from Hell'.

Blackbeard's real name was Edward Teach (or Thatch). He was probably born in Bristol in around 1680, although some sources claim that he came from Jamaica or Carolina. Nothing is known for certain of his early life, although he is said to have been a privateer during the War of the Spanish Succession. If so, he would have been one of the thousands of seamen who lost their jobs, when peace was agreed in 1713. Many of these decided that piracy was their best option and gravitated to the Caribbean. It was there, in New Providence, that Teach's activities were first recorded. He had teamed up with a minor freebooter called Benjamin Hornigold who was, as it were, teaching him his trade.

Teach's association with Hornigold did not last long. Towards the end of 1716, they took three vessels, relieving them of their cargoes of wine and flour. Then, in the following spring, they captured a large Guineaman heading for Martinique. Teach took an instant liking to the ship and decided to make it his own. Wisely, Hornigold agreed. The apprenticeship was over.

After taking command of his new vessel, Teach's first act was to change its name to the *Queen Anne's Revenge*. In common with many of his fellow rovers, he hated the new Hanoverian dynasty, which had ascended to the English throne in 1714, largely because King George had expressed his desire to rid the seas of pirates. Accordingly, Blackbeard's ship was named in honour of the previous monarch (Queen Anne, reigned 1702-14).

It did not take long before Teach's skills were put to

the test. Shortly afterwards, he ran into H.M.S. *Scarborough*, a British man-of-war, captained by Francis Hume. The latter had already enjoyed some success in his mission against the pirates, capturing two renegade sloops, and he immediately attacked Blackbeard's ship. The two vessels exchanged fire for several hours, before Hume gave up the attempt and retired to his base in Barbados.

If Blackbeard could hold off a fully-armed British warship, then it is hardly surprising that he was able to overcome most merchant ships with ease. He now embarked on a reign of terror, which reached its peak in May 1718, when he blockaded the port of Charleston in South Carolina. Anchoring just outside the harbour, Blackbeard waylaid each new ship as it arrived, seizing goods and hostages. Within the space of just one week, nine vessels had fallen victim to this ploy. The richest prize was the *Crowley*, which was carrying a substantial amount of money, together with a member of the governor's council, Samuel Wragg, and his four-year-old son. By now, the authorities in Charleston were desperate. Trade was at a standstill, with crews too frightened to sail their ships in or out of port. Worse still, Blackbeard was threatening to kill his hostages and send the heads of Wragg and his son to the governor, unless his demands were met. Inevitably, they caved in and heaved a collective sigh of relief, when the pirate finally sailed away.

Blackbeard terrified his own men, every bit as much as his victims. On one occasion, after there had been talk of his devilish ways, he decided to create his own version of hell and challenged his men, to see if any of them could bear it longer than him. A few took up the gauntlet, joining Blackbeard in the hold, where they closed all the hatches and set light to some brimstone. As the suffocating fumes filled the air, they were soon crying to be let out, while the pirate captain remained seated and scoffed at their weakness.

This was by no means Blackbeard's most extreme

outburst. On a separate occasion, he was drinking below deck with his sailing master, Israel Hands, and another man. Stealthily, he drew out two guns underneath the table. Then, without warning, he blew out the candle, crossed his hands over and fired two shots into the dark. One of them tore into Israel's knee, maiming him permanently. This pointless act of brutality was a chilling example of Blackbeard's twisted sense of humour. He dismissed it by remarking of his crew that, 'if he did not now and then kill one of them, they would forget who he was'.

Not surprisingly, Hands never forgave Blackbeard. He later deserted and turned king's evidence, speaking out against the pirate's atrocities. This earned him a pardon, but the injury put an end to his working life and he ended his days begging on the streets of London. He would have been astonished to learn that his name would become more famous after his death, thanks to *Treasure Island*. It caught the eye of Stevenson, as he was reading Captain Johnson's book, and he decided to use Israel Hands as a character in his novel. In it, Hands was the wicked coxswain, who fought with Jim Hawkins. It has also been suggested that his fate as a beggar may have helped to inspire the character of Blind Pew.

In spite of his ruthlessness, Blackbeard got on well enough with his fellow pirate captains. There was a mutual (if wary) respect between Charles Vane and himself, and he occasionally operated alongside other adventurers. These included Stede Bonnet, one of the most eccentric members of the pirate community. Although the term is often overused, Bonnet was a genuine 'gentleman' pirate. He was a wealthy landowner from Barbados, rather than a former sailor or privateer, and he had enjoyed a successful career in the army, reaching the rank of major. To the amazement of his friends and family, Bonnet abandoned his respectable lifestyle, bought and fitted out his own sloop, and embarked on a new career as a pirate. The reason for this bizarre decision, according to Captain Johnson, was that he was desperate to escape his nagging wife.

Despite his inexperience, Bonnet fared well enough at the outset. He captured a number of ships off the coast of New England and Virginia, before teaming up with Blackbeard for a series of joint attacks. However, Teach had his doubts about the competence of this bookish man, who seemed to spend too much time reading in his cabin or wandering around the deck in his morning coat, and he eventually installed one of his own men as the captain of Bonnet's ship. It is true that he later restored the command to him temporarily, although this was part of one of his ruses.

Blackbeard was always on the lookout for fine ships to add to his collection. At one stage, he led a fleet of six vessels, with over 400 men under his command. His greatest prize, perhaps, was a French slaver, called the

Concorde, which he spotted in November 1717, to the east of Martinique. In theory, slave ships were more powerful than other merchant vessels - they had larger crews and more guns. In reality, however, they could sometimes present an easy target. The conditions on board were generally unsanitary and disease-ridden, affecting both the crew and their wretched human cargo, so resistance could be minimal. This was the case with the *Concorde*, where the sailors had been laid low by scurvy and dysentery. As soon as the pirates attacked, the French captain struck his colours and surrendered. The *Concorde* proved to be an even richer prize than Blackbeard had anticipated, as its luckless commander was carrying a secret cargo of gold, silver plate, and jewellery, which the pirates gleefully removed.

By the summer of 1718, Blackbeard was at the peak of his career. He had money, he had ships, and he had the type of reputation he had always craved. He was the most notorious pirate operating on the high seas, feared throughout the American colonies and the West Indies. It was hard to see how he could improve his situation any further, but Blackbeard had a plan and, in the autumn of 1718, he started to carry it out. The effects would be devastating, both for him and for all the pirates in the Caribbean.

THE WAR
AGAINST THE PIRATES

HE TIDE BEGAN TO TURN against piracy in the early 18th
century, when the political situation in Europe
changed. In 1713, the War of the Spanish Succession
(1702-13) finally came to an end. This had the unfortunate side-effect of creating a dramatic rise in unemploy-
ment amongst sailors and privateers. In two years, the
British navy was cut by over 30,000 men. For many of
these, piracy seemed the obvious alternative. The mount-
ing crime wave, coupled with a desire to re-open old trade
routes, prompted the authorities on both sides of the
Atlantic to take action. Letters of marque were not
renewed and governments were no longer prepared to
turn a blind eye to the problem.

Initially, there were attempts to solve the problem
through legislation. The first steps had already been taken
in 1700, with the introduction of the Act for the More
Effectual Suppression of Piracy. This addressed a long-
standing legal anomaly, which meant that pirates had to
be shipped back to England for their trial. The long delays
that this involved, coupled with the fact that any hangings
would be carried out far away on Execution Dock,
severely undermined any deterrent value that might be
gained in the Americas.

One of the first men to fall foul of the new legislation
was the mutineer, John Quelch. He took command of the

Charles, after the crew rebelled against its captain, and led his men in a series of raids against shipping off the coast of Brazil. The reports of these attacks provide one of the first records of a pirate hoisting the 'Old Roger'. Quelch's personal device was 'an anatomy [a skeleton] with an hour-glass in one hand and in the other a dart with three drops of blood proceeding from it'.

When Quelch was apprehended in 1704, he was tried and executed with six of his men in Boston. The hangings took place by the water's edge and drew large crowds. One witness estimated that about a hundred boats clustered near the spot and 'when the scaffold was let to sink, there was such a screech of the women that my wife heard it sitting in...our orchard, a full mile from the place'. Although it horrified some, the authorities hoped that this gory spectacle would set an example and deter other villains from following the same course.

In spite of these tough measures, the situation continued to deteriorate. More unemployed seamen turned to piracy, encouraged by the sensational reports in the newspapers about the latest atrocities committed on the high seas. This state of affairs became even worse, when Blackbeard and Charles Vane arrived on the scene.

Eventually, the new regime - George I had come to the throne in 1714 - decided that more drastic action was needed. In 1718, Woodes Rogers, a tough ex-privateer, was sent out to the Bahamas as the new governor, to clean up one of the most notorious pirate haunts. Rogers was already a well-known figure. His chief commission as a privateer had been a lengthy voyage around the world (1708-11), sponsored by the Lord High Admiral and the Mayor of Bristol. He swiftly proved his mettle as a captain, surviving through a number of mutinies and storms, and returning home with a fabulous haul of gold, precious stones, and luxurious textiles. Rogers wrote an account of his journey, *A Cruising Voyage Round the World*, which became a bestseller after its publication in 1712. He little realised it, but one incident from this expedition was to go down in history, for in 1709 he rescued Alexander Selkirk - the model for Robinson Crusoe (see p.33) - from his solitary life on a desert island.

At the same time, the king backed up the appointment of Rogers by declaring an amnesty, promising a pardon to any pirate who surrendered to the authorities. This was a bold, but highly controversial move. Many pirates responded to the new initiative, though some were reluctant to hand over their loot, while others simply returned to a life of piracy, after receiving their pardon.

BENJAMIN HORNIGOLD

Blackbeard's old mentor, Benjamin Hornigold, was one of those who decided to accept the pardon. In common with a number of his former colleagues, he was promptly recruited by the authorities to track down any pirates who remained at large. On the orders of Woodes Rogers, he was immediately sent out to apprehend Charles Vane, one of the most troublesome offenders.

Vane was far too slippery a customer to fall into Hornigold's grasp, but the pirate-hunter did not return empty-handed. On the island of Exuma, he arrested a group of rovers, who had accepted the royal pardon, but lapsed back into piracy. One of the men, John Augur, had been master of the *Mary*, but the remainder came from lesser ranks. These captives could not be viewed as high profile villains, by any stretch of the imagination, but Rogers was determined to make an example of them. Ten men were brought to trial and eight of these were condemned to death. Within two days of the sentence, the executions were carried out, in front of the fortress at Nassau. Rogers hoped that the speed and the severity of his measures would send out a message of intent to all the other pirates operating in the Caribbean. He now had to wait nervously, to see if this ploy would succeed.

MAJOR STEDE BONNET

Like Hornigold, Bonnet decided to accept the royal pardon, even though he had no intention of honouring its

conditions. Bonnet was still a member of Blackbeard's party at this stage but, while he was away making his pledge, the pirate captain ransacked his ship and abandoned him.

Bonnet swore revenge, but Blackbeard was already long gone, so instead he returned to his pirating ways. For a brief while, he enjoyed some success, seizing goods from 13 ships, but his luck soon ran out. During one of the confrontations, his vessel was damaged and he was forced to look for shelter in an inlet of Cape Fear River, while he carried out repairs. Before these were completed, however, Bonnet was cornered by one of the pirate-hunters, Colonel William Rhett.

Rhett had actually been searching for Charles Vane, but he was happy enough to find Bonnet. The major was taken back to Charleston, where he was put on trial with his crew. During the proceedings, Bonnet's education and his respectable background were held against him, making his crimes all the more despicable. After he was sentenced to death, he made a desperate plea to the governor, asking for the amputation of 'all my Limbs from my Body, only reserving the Use of my Tongue, to call continually on, and pray to the Lord'. This plea fell on deaf ears and he was hanged on the waterfront at Charleston, along with 29 members of his crew.

CHARLES VANE

Rogers had been told that there were a thousand pirates waiting for him in New Providence, ready and willing to accept the royal pardon. If he truly believed that his job would be that simple, he soon learned otherwise. As his fleet approached the harbour, it was greeted by loud blasts and flashes of fiery light. The culprit was Charles Vane, who had loaded an old French sloop with explosives, set it alight, and then sent it drifting towards the new arrivals. Rogers immediately sent out two ships to apprehend the villain, but Vane outdistanced them with ease and made his escape.

Charles Vane was the scourge of Caribbean shipping. He operated in the same period and in the same areas as his friend and rival, Blackbeard. He was at least as successful as the latter and might even have become more famous, had he shared Blackbeard's gift for self-publicity. He certainly possessed the same ruthless streak, when it came to getting information out of his victims. When he captured the *Edward and Mary* in April 1718, he ordered his men to put lighted matches to the eyes of the crew, while he himself pushed the muzzle of a loaded pistol into the captain's mouth, so that they would reveal the hiding-place of any loot. On the very same day, Vane also attacked another sloop, the *Diamond*. On this occasion, one of the crew was singled out and strung up by his neck, to encourage the others to speak. Then, when the raid was over, the *Diamond* was set alight.

During the remainder of the year, Vane cruised round the Windward Islands, before turning his attention to the American colonies. He enjoyed particular success operating off the Carolina coast, near Charleston, and then further north, near New York. For much of this time, he worked with two ships, exchanging vessels whenever he captured a larger or more powerful one. Vane suffered a temporary setback in November, when he was ousted from his command by Calico Jack (see p.10), but he retained the loyalty of several followers and was soon back in business. Within a month, he had captured three new vessels, while cruising off the coast of Jamaica. As he wintered on the island of Bonacca (now Guanaja), Vane was convinced that his position was as strong as ever.

In common with Sam Bellamy, Vane's eventual down-fall owed more to the forces of nature than to the British efforts at policing. In February 1719, he ran into a

tornado and was shipwrecked on a tiny island, in the Bay of Honduras. He was trapped there in a miserable state, until he was finally picked up by a reformed buccaneer, who promptly turned him over to the authorities in Jamaica. Vane was tried there in March 1720 and sentenced to hang. After this, his corpse was squeezed into an iron cage and displayed at the gibbet on Gun Cay, near Port Royal.

──The Downfall of Blackbeard──

Where Blackbeard was concerned, there was no honour
amongst thieves. He felt no compunction at all about
stealing from his own men or any other pirates. So, when
his company had amassed a considerable amount of
booty, he decided it was time to slim down his operation,
before a share-out could take place. He deliberately
grounded two of his ships at Topsail Inlet (now Beaufort
Inlet) in North Carolina, taking care to make this seem
like an accident. He then instructed the crewmen from
these two vessels to proceed up the coast on foot, promising to pick them up later. At the same time, he also
persuaded Stede Bonnet to leave his ship - which had
only recently been restored to him - in order to arrange a
pardon for himself. By the time he returned, of course,
Blackbeard had absconded with all the loot from this and
the two grounded vessels.

Blackbeard now established a new base at Ocracoke
Inlet, just offshore from the town of Bath in North
Carolina. This was a shrewd decision. At the time,
the state had limited maritime trade and was more
welcoming than most to the pirates. In addition,
Blackbeard had befriended the local governor, Charles
Eden, who issued him with a pardon and allowed him to
offload his stolen goods, in return for a share of the
proceeds. Better still, the shallow waters and narrow
channels of Ocracoke were effectively impassable for
large warships, so the hideout offered the pirate considerable, natural protection.

With these crucial factors in his favour, Blackbeard
felt secure. He could go out on raids, from time to time,
and still enjoy his ill-gotten gains at his leisure.
Unfortunately for him, this arrangement was less than
popular with the governors of the neighbouring colonies.
One of these, Alexander Spotswood, the governor of

Virginia, decided to take action. He conferred secretly
with the captains of two British men-of-war, the *Lyme* and
the *Pearl*, and agreed to hire small sloops for them, so that
they could pursue Blackbeard into his lair. At the same
time, he persuaded his council to pass an act 'to
Encourage the Apprehending and Destroying of Pirates',
which offered generous rewards for the capture of any
pirates 'within one hundred leagues of the Continent of
Virginia'. The legality of these moves was highly ques-
tionable, as Spotswood had no jurisdiction whatsoever in
North Carolina, but he was convinced that the chance of
catching Blackbeard was worth the risk.

The two navy sloops set out on November 17, 1718,
with Lieutenant Maynard in command. Blackbeard heard
of their approach, but made no effort to escape, perhaps
because most of his crew was ashore, in Bath. When
Maynard eventually confronted the pirate on the morning
of November 21, Blackbeard had just 18 men with him.
In addition, his senses were probably dulled, after an all-
night drinking session with the master of a local sloop.
Nevertheless, he remained defiant, calling out to
Maynard: 'Damnation seize my soul if I give you quarter,
or take any from you!' With this, he fired a devastating
broadside, which caused carnage on the navy sloop.

In order to prevent a repetition of this, Maynard
ordered most of his men to take shelter in the hold. He
remained alone on deck, accompanied only by his pilot
and helmsman. This fooled Blackbeard into thinking that
the guns had done their work, so he boarded the sloop
with his followers. At this stage, Maynard's men clam-
bered out of the hold and a desperate fight ensued.
Blackbeard realized his mistake, but still fought like a
man possessed. He exchanged pistol fire with the lieutenant, before engaging him in swordplay. Maynard's
weapon buckled, as it struck the pirate's cartridge box,
and Blackbeard immediately broke the blade. He was
about to despatch the disarmed seaman, when one of

Maynard's men - a highlander - came to his rescue, carving a deep wound in Blackbeard's neck with his cutlass. This proved to be the fatal blow. Blackbeard finally collapsed on the deck, which was already running with blood and gore. Maynard later reported that the pirate chief had suffered no fewer than 25 wounds - that he 'fell with five Shot in him, and 20 dismal Cuts in several Parts of his Body'. After the battle, he attached Blackbeard's head to the bowsprit of his ship, displaying it as a grisly trophy of his victory. The pirate's headless body was heaved unceremoniously over the side where, according to local legend, it proceeded to swim around the sloop several times.

The battle did not end with Blackbeard's death, as his followers doubtless knew that they would be shown little mercy at any trial. In the end, 15 pirates were taken back to Williamsburg, among them some of the men who had been ashore in Bath and had missed the fight. The propaganda value of Maynard's triumph was slightly marred by the lengthy, legal wrangles that ensued. Blackbeard's men did not stand trial until March, when all but two were sentenced to hang, while the squabbles over Governor Eden's collusion and Maynard's reward went on far longer. The latter had to wait four years for a final decision, when the total amount shared out came to just over £334. In a shameful display of ingratitude, the authorities cut the reward money, because Blackbeard had not been taken alive.

BARTHOLOMEW ROBERTS

Although his fame has been eclipsed by that of Blackbeard, many would consider that Bartholomew Roberts - better known as 'Black Bart' - was the most successful pirate of his age. In common with many of his colleagues, his career was comparatively brief but, in under four years, he captured more than 400 vessels and terrorised the shipping of three continents.

Roberts was born near Haverfordwest, in Wales, in 1682. He trained as a merchant seaman and was serving as second mate on a slaver, the *Princess*, when his life suddenly changed direction. In 1719, his ship was taken by another Welshman, Howel Davis, and he was invited to join their pirate crew. It is unclear if Roberts was willing to follow this path but, in any event, his skills must have impressed his new shipmates. For, just six weeks later, Davis was killed in an ambush and Roberts was elected captain.

He wasted little time in proving his mettle. Soon his new ship, the *Royal Rover*, was bound for the coast of Brazil, where a rich prize awaited them. In Bahia harbour, they came across a fleet of around 40 Portuguese merchantmen, with an escort of two warships idling nearby. Without hesitation, Roberts advanced into the heart of the flotilla, seeking out the most heavily laden prize. While the other ships looked helplessly on, his men ransacked the ship, making off with 40,000 gold moidores

Bartholomew Roberts, otherwise known as 'Black Bart'

(worth around £50,000), a valuable cargo of sugar, hides, and tobacco, and a diamond cross that was meant for the king of Portugal.

This daring raid was not an isolated incident. In the summer of 1720, Roberts launched a similar attack on a fleet of ships in the harbour of Trepassey, in Newfoundland. By this stage, the pirate was so infamous that he did not even need to fire a shot. He raised his black flag and had his musicians create a wild cacophony of noise with their horns and drums. The sailors fled in terror, leaving Roberts and his men to plunder the ships at their leisure. After they had finished, they set fire to most of the vessels, apart from a Bristol galley, which was renamed the *Royal Fortune* and added to the pirate fleet.

With bold forays of this kind, it was not long before the Welshman's name was feared in every port and harbour. Roberts' unusual character added to his notoriety. He cut an imposing figure as a 'gentleman' pirate, dressed in a crimson damask waistcoat and breeches, with a gold chain around his neck, and a tricorne hat adorned with a red feather. Almost uniquely for a pirate he did not consume alcohol, preferring to drink tea. Roberts also tried to maintain discipline by drawing up a set of articles, which every member of his crew had to sign. Many of the clauses were conventional enough, with rules for the sharing out of loot and the penalties for desertion, but Roberts also banned any gambling with dice or cards, and set limits on the times that his men could drink.

Roberts' attacks were as varied as they were audacious. One of the main reasons why the authorities took so long to catch him was the fact that he kept moving. His activities ranged along much of the eastern seaboard of North and South America, as well as the coastline of West Africa. In the Caribbean alone, he bombarded the stronghold at St. Kitts and devastated the shipping routes around Barbados, Martinique, Bermuda, and St. Lucia.

His luck finally ran out in February 1722, when he was cruising along the west African coast near Cape Lopez (now part of Gabon). Here, he was tracked by two British warships, the *Swallow* and the *Weymouth*. Roberts made the fatal error of mistaking the former for a large merchant vessel. As the two ships exchanged fire, a blast of grapeshot tore out his throat, killing him instantly. While the battle was still raging, his men carried out the instructions he had always given them and cast his body over the side, still dressed in all its fine attire.

Without their charismatic captain, Roberts' crew surrendered tamely and were taken to Cape Coast Castle, a major slave-trading post (now in Ghana). There, they were imprisoned in the slave hole, to await their trial. In all, 169 men were charged. Of these, 52 were condemned

PIRATE TRIALS, 1715-25

Date and Location / Pirates / Outcome

November 1715, London
Capt. Dolzell
Hanged at Execution Dock

June 1717, Charleston
Ernandos, De Cossey, Rossoe, and De Mont
All four were hanged

October 1717, Boston
Eight survivors from Sam Bellamy's shipwrecked crew
Six were hanged

December 1717, Nassau
Ten pirates captured by Capt. Hornigold
Eight were hanged

October 1718, Charleston
Major Stede Bonnet
Thirty hanged, including Bonnet himself

1719, London
Laws, Tyril, and Cadiz
All three hanged at Execution Dock

February 1719, Charleston
Capt. Worley
Hanged

March 1719, Williamsburg
15 of Blackbeard's men
13 were hanged. Israel Hands was reprieved

November 1720, Spanish Town, Jamaica
Jack Rackham and his crew
Ten executed, including Rackham himself

November 1720, Spanish Town, Jamaica
Mary Read and Anne Bonny
Guilty but not hanged, as they were both pregnant

March 1721, Spanish Town, Jamaica
Capt. Charles Vane
Hanged at Gallows Point

1722, Jamaica
Capt. Luke and 41 men hanged

March 1722, Cape Coast Castle, West Africa
Bartholomew Roberts' crew
52 hanged, 74 acquitted, 37 imprisoned

October 1722, Nassau
Capt. Blanco's crew
Five men executed

July 1723, London
Capt. Massey Hanged at Execution Dock

July 1723, Newport, Rhode Island
Capt. Harris and crew
26 men hanged

July 1723, London
Capt. Philip Roche
Hanged at Execution Dock

1723, Antigua
Capt. Finn and five men hanged

March 1724, St. Kitts
Capt. Lowther's crew
Eleven men hanged

May 1724, Boston
Capt. Archer and crew
Archer hanged on Bird Island

May 1725, London
Capt. Gow and crew
Ten hanged at Execution Dock,
including Gow

to death, 74 were acquitted, and the remainder were sentenced to imprisonment or hard labour. The executions took place, a few at a time, on the castle ramparts. The hangings went on for a fortnight, and 18 of the worst offenders were 'sun-dried' in iron cages, at prominent spots along the coast.

The downfall of Bartholomew Roberts is often said to mark the end of the golden age of piracy. He was the last of the great marauders to remain at liberty, and the mass executions proved a powerful deterrent to pirates in the Caribbean and elsewhere.

Major Stede Bonnet hanged at Charleston, 1718

THE PIRATE IMAGE

BY THE TIME that Robert Louis Stevenson (1850-94) came to write *Treasure Island*, the general public had some very firm preconceptions about pirates. Stevenson was keen to exploit these, writing excitedly to a friend about his new book: 'If this don't fetch the kids, why, they have gone rotten since my day. Will you be surprised to learn that it is about Buccaneers...that it's all about a map and a treasure and a mutiny and a derelict ship...and a Sea Cook with one leg, and a sea song with the chorus "Yo-ho-ho and a bottle of Rum".' The same clichés about pirates are still in circulation today, some of them true, while others are highly fanciful.

THE JOLLY ROGER

The origin of the pirates' famous flag, displaying a skull and crossbones, is still uncertain. One popular theory is that the name comes from *jolie rouge* (French for 'red beauty'). Some of the older pirate flags were red, symbolising the bloodthirsty intentions of the raiders. Another possibility is that it was a corruption of 'Old Roger', a slang term for the devil.

The Jolly Roger was by no means the only pirate flag. Some captains replaced the crossbones with a pair of cutlasses, or added a skeleton, a wounded heart, or an hourglass. All of these proclaimed the imminent death of the pirates' victims. Some flags were highly personal.

Bartholomew Roberts flew one, which portrayed him standing triumphantly on two skulls. These were labelled ABH (A Barbados Head) and AMH (A Martinique Head), to symbolise his feud with the authorities on these two islands.

The purpose of the flags was to intimidate the crew of the ship under attack, in the hope that they would surrender without a fight. Pirates were naturally keen to win their prize with as little trouble as possible. In addition, they sometimes planned to steal the ship itself and hoped, if possible, to seize it without causing any unnecessary damage.

BURIED TREASURE

This is almost as much of a myth as the treasure map. In the first place, it would be wrong to imagine that every ship attacked by pirates was heavily laden with pieces of eight and gold doubloons. Most vessels carried mundane cargoes that were of little or no use to pirates. In addition, the majority of these adventurers lived very much for the moment. Most were young men, who were well aware that their career was likely to be brief and would probably end with them 'drying in the sun', hanging from the gallows in Execution Dock. As a result, they spent their money quickly, drinking and whoring in their favourite haunts in New Providence and Port Royal.

Legends about pirate treasure have always been plentiful, often arising while the rogues were still at liberty. Some of these stemmed from sensational news reports or fanciful ballads, while others were inspired by the details of stolen booty, mentioned in pirate trials. Both during his lifetime and in later years, the most celebrated stories concerned Captain Kidd. The riches that he had plundered from the *Quedagh Merchant* were widely publicised and Kidd added fuel to these rumours by making extravagant attempts to bribe officials, as his plight became more desperate. When he was in Newgate Prison, for example, he wrote to the Speaker of the House of Commons, offering (in vain) to hand over £100,000 to the government, if he could be sent under guard to retrieve it.

Almost certainly, Kidd's treasure did not exist. The

accounts of his booty were wildly exaggerated and, in addition, a substantial amount was recovered at the time of his arrest. This has not deterred treasure-hunters from speculating about the potential hiding-place of any further loot. The most popular theory is that he concealed it somewhere on Gardiner's Island, not far from New York, shortly after learning that he had been declared a pirate. Other suggested locations include Sayville on Long Island, Clarke's Island in the Connecticut River, and Oak Island in Nova Scotia. Some of the theorists claim to have found mysterious, coded charts, but no one has actually discovered any treasure.

TREASURE MAP

This is effectively an invention of Robert Louis Stevenson. In the summer of 1881, the author was staying with his family at Braemar, in Scotland. It rained for much of the time, so for long periods they had to amuse themselves indoors. Together with Lloyd, his twelve-year-old stepson, he drew a map of a mysterious island, where there was buried treasure. Stevenson later admitted that it was this map, which first gave him the idea of writing *Treasure Island*. Sadly, the original map was lost in transit to the publishers, so the author had a copy drawn up in his father's office.

PIECES OF EIGHT

Made famous by Long John Silver's parrot, which was taught to cry out 'Pieces of Eight', this was a genuine type of coin. The Spanish dollar or peso was effectively the universal currency, during the heyday of the Caribbean pirates. It was worth eight *reales* and bore the figure '8' on one side. This large coin was frequently cut into eight pieces, in order to provide small change. These fragments were known colloquially as 'pieces of eight'.

WALKING THE PLANK

It is a tribute to the power of popular culture that, when most people think of pirates, the first thing that comes to mind is 'walking the plank'. According to tradition, this punishment was first devised by Stede Bonnet, but there is no evidence at all to support this claim. In fact, very few instances of walking the plank have ever been recorded, all of them long after the golden age of piracy. The best-known example was reported in *The Times* of July 23, 1829, when 30 pirates boarded a Dutch vessel in the Caribbean and forced its crew to walk the plank. The unfortunate men were blindfolded, had their arms pinioned, and had weights attached to their feet.

The image of walking the plank was popularised through a much-reproduced illustration by Howard Pyle, which first appeared in *Harper's Weekly* in 1887. There is no doubt, however, that the perennial success of *Peter Pan* - where Captain Hook threatens to make the lost boys walk the plank - bears the chief responsibility for keeping the idea in the public eye.

Pirates had mixed attitudes to violence. Most were happy to avoid it, if their prey surrendered without a fight, and there are many recorded instances of pirate captains displaying great magnanimity towards their victims. Yet, of course, they were equally capable of immense brutality. Rather than make their enemies walk the plank, they would simply throw them overboard, if they had no further use for them. Acts of cruelty or torture could also be useful, if they loosened tongues about the hidden location of any valuable cargo. One of the most common torments was 'woolding', where a thin cord was wound so tightly around a victim's head that his eyes burst out of his skull. The term was borrowed from the everyday task of binding cords around a mast.

In any event, the cruelty of some pirates has to be viewed in context. Most of them went to sea initially as legitimate sailors, where they were subject to a very strict code of discipline. The savage floggings and keel-haulings that were a fact of life on many ships were every bit as brutal as the punishments meted out by pirates.

WOODEN LEGS

The popular image of pirates with wooden legs and eye-patches is firmly based on reality. Injuries were commonplace and, as surgical facilities were very limited, victims were often permanently maimed. On a ship under the command of a certain Captain Phillips, there was no surgeon at all and amputations were carried out by the ship's carpenter, Thomas Fern. The scale of injury problems is illustrated by the fact that most pirate 'articles' specified various grades of compensation payments, that would be due to any man who suffered a serious injury, or the loss of a limb, when going into action.

In pirate fiction, the most famous amputee was Long John Silver, in *Treasure Island*. He did not actually have a wooden leg, but moved around with the use of a crutch, which could also serve as a weapon. Stevenson based the character on his friend, the writer and editor W.E. Henley (1849-1903), who had lost a foot during his childhood. In the novel, Silver changed jobs, becoming a cook rather than a quartermaster after his operation. This was an authentic detail, as many real-life pirates took on similar posts, in order to remain at sea after becoming crippled.

PARROTS

Pirates have been associated with parrots and other exotic pets, ever since *Treasure Island*. This featured the most famous parrot in literary history - Cap'n Flint. She liked to perch on the shoulder of Long John Silver and, according to him, had once belonged to another (real-life) pirate, Captain England. When she was not swearing, Silver's bird would cry 'pieces of eight', echoing her owner's obsession with treasure. The idea of pirates owning pets of this kind was a perfectly authentic detail. They were genuinely fond of picking up unusual birds and animals on their travels. Parrots were a particular favourite, as there was a ready market for them back in England. In 1717, one London paper advertised 'Parrokeets which talk English, Dutch, French, and Spanish, Whistle at command...very tame and pretty'.

THE PIRATE CODE

It is often claimed that, for all their greed and brutality, the communities on pirate ships were more democratic and egalitarian than any government. There is some truth in this. Pirate captains were elected by the crew and could be deposed by them. Even a successful leader like Charles Vane suffered this indignity. The captain and his officers had the same rations as their men and, while they normally got a larger share of any booty, the precise division of the spoils was worked out and agreed in advance. Crews could vote on the region where the ship was to operate, and there was even a primitive social security system, with compensation payments for men who lost a limb or were disabled during a raid. On many day-to-day issues, the quartermaster had more power than the

TYPICAL CLAUSES IN THE ARTICLES OF A PIRATE SHIP

1 Every man shall obey civil command. The Captain shall have one full share and a half in all prizes. The master carpenter, boatswain, and gunner [known as 'artists'] shall have one share and a quarter.

2 If any man shall run away or keep any secret from the company, he shall be marooned with one bottle of powder, one bottle of water, one small arm and shot.

3 If any man steal anything in the company, or game, to the value of a piece of eight, he shall be marooned or shot.

4 Any man that shall not keep his arms clean, fit for an engagement, or neglect his business, shall be cut off from his share and suffer such other punishment as the captain and the company shall think fit.

5 If any man shall lose a joint in time of an engagement, he shall have 400 pieces of eight; if a limb, 800.

captain. Only during an attack could he command absolute authority.

All of these matters were written down in a set of articles or regulations, governing conduct on board the ship. In theory, this arrangement sounds democratic, but there were plenty of exceptions. Most mutinies were, in effect, violent coups that took place without any voting, and there was nothing very democratic about the way that many of the pirates' victims were pressed into their service. Captains were always on the lookout for skilled men, such as carpenters, coopers, or musicians, and often threatened these prisoners with torture or death, if they did not join the crew. In spite of these menaces, many 'forced men' were later tried and hanged as pirates. On top of this, most captains were willing to resort to brutal measures, in order to maintain discipline amongst their men. In Drake's day, typical punishments included cutting off a hand (for drawing a knife on an officer), covering a man's scalp with boiling oil and feathers (for stealing), and marooning (for falling asleep on watch).

COLOURFUL COSTUMES

Most seamen, whether pirates or law-abiding sailors, dressed differently from landlubbers. The arduous, physical tasks that formed part of everyday maritime life meant that tough, hard-wearing clothes were required. Short blue jackets and canvas trousers were the norm. However, many pirate captains gained a reputation for wearing luxurious finery, stolen from their victims. John Rackham, for example, was widely known as 'Calico Jack', because of his taste for wearing garish cotton clothes, while Kit Oloard sported black velvet trousers, crimson silk socks, and a large felt hat. As the clothes were stolen, however, they were often ill-fitting, so the overall effect was outlandish, rather than stylish.

Many pirates did wear a broad sash across their chest, to which they attached as many pistols as they could carry. This was an entirely practical measure, as there was no time to stop and reload a gun during the heat of battle.

The swashbuckling reputation of pirate costumes has won them lasting popularity. Pirate outfits are still a firm favourite at children's fancy dress parties, and the pirate style has also been taken up by famous couturiers. In the 1980s, New Romantic fashions were pioneered by Vivienne Westwood, using her 'Pirates' collection. This was launched in her Kings Road shop, which was fitted out to resemble a storm-tossed galleon, and was then shown on the catwalk in March 1981.

THE CUTLASS

This distinctive sword was the pirate's weapon of choice. It was a short, broad sword, with a single cutting edge. The blade could be straight or slightly curved, and the hilt normally took the form of a basket-shaped guard. The weapon was popular at sea, because it was strong enough to cut through rope and canvas, but was also short enough for use in hand-to-hand fighting. Traditionally, the cutlass is said to have developed from the long knives, used by the buccaneers to skewer their meat, but most historians remain unconvinced about this. Cutlasses were worn by some members of the British Royal Navy until as late as 1941.

Of course, the cutlass was not a pirate's only weapon. When attacking another ship, most would also have carried pistols, a dagger, and a boarding axe (for cutting nets and rigging). Many pirates also made use of a primitive type of grenade. These were known as granado shells or grenadoes, after the Spanish word for 'pomegranate' (*grenada*). The devices, which were hollow balls filled with gunpowder, were thrown at the enemy just prior to boarding.

MAROONING

For every mariner, the thought of being abandoned on a lonely desert isle was a haunting prospect. Some pirate chiefs played on this fear by turning it into a cruel punishment. Mutinous crew members or unwanted captives were deliberately marooned on remote islands. There, they were obliged to live off the land, or else face a lingering death from starvation.

In pirate fiction, the most famous character to suffer this fate was Ben Gunn, in *Treasure Island*. Marooning, however, was not a literary invention. In real life, the most celebrated victim was a Scottish privateer called Alexander Selkirk (1680-1721). In 1703 he joined an expedition to the South Seas, but in the following year, after quarrelling with the ship's master, he and his possessions were put ashore on a tiny island, off the coast of Chile. Selkirk was stranded there until 1709, living mainly off wild goats. His ordeal made him famous, providing the inspiration for Defoe's *Robinson Crusoe* (1719). Ironically, the pilot of the boat which rescued him was the buccaneer and explorer, William Dampier, who had been a member of the crew on Selkirk's ill-fated, privateering voyage.

FIFTEEN MEN ON THE DEAD MAN'S CHEST — YO-HO-HO, AND A BOTTLE OF RUM —

There has been much speculation about this couplet, which appears at the start of *Treasure Island*. Attempts have been made to link it to a genuine sea shanty, but without success. Stevenson gave the game away in a letter to his friend, W.E. Henley, where he described it as 'a real Buccaneer's song, only known to the crew of the late Captain Flint' - in other words, he invented it for his fictitious character. Stevenson also mentioned that he took

'Dead Man's Chest' from a travel book by Charles
Kingsley, where it was identified as one of the Virgin
Islands. In 1901, however, Allison and Waller added new
lyrics and turned the couplet into a song for a Broadway
musical.

PIRATE PROVISIONS

For much of the time, pirates did not eat as well or as
regularly as their counterparts in the navy or on merchant
ships. By the nature of their calling, there were times
when food was very scarce. So, whenever a ship was
captured, they were quick to rifle its stores and provisions.
Rum and tobacco were the chief priorities. Even
Blackbeard became concerned about the loyalty of his
crew, when rum was in short supply. This also explains
why pirate sloops often raided small fishing boats.

Bumboe	A type of rum punch, made from cane liquor and spices.
Dough-boys	Boiled dumplings, often cooked in sea-water, to avoid wasting precious stocks of fresh water.
Flip	A warm concoction of beer, rum, and sugar.
Grog	A sailor's ration of watered-down rum.
Pickled shark	Fish was obviously a staple part of the seaman's diet. Snapper, catfish, herring, salt cod, and albacore were all popular, although any fish that could be pickled and pre served was useful. William Dampier's favourite dish was shark pickled with pepper and vinegar.
Salmagundi	A spicy stew of minced meat or

fish, marinated in wine, combined with such items as hard-boiled eggs, anchovies, pickled herring, cabbage, mangoes, or pickled vegetables. In England, the name became corrupted to 'solomon-gundy' and it is probably related to the children's rhyme *Solomon Grundy*.

Ship's biscuits These lasted well during long voyages, but they were rock-hard and prone to infestation by black-headed weevils. Also known as hard tack. When mixed with bacon grease, they produced a sticky concoction called skillygalee.

Tobacco Regarded by pirates as an essential element of their provisions. Used to stave off hunger in lean times. Generally smoked in long-stemmed, clay pipes.

Turtles In the Caribbean, pirates considered the meat of the sea-tortoise or turtle a rare delicacy. In 1704, one visitor to Jamaica noted that 'The flesh looks and eats much like choice veal, but the fat is of a green colour, very luscious and sweet; the liver is likewise green, very wholesome, searching and purging.' Better still, the creatures could be kept alive in the ship's hold until required, so the meat would be fresh.

There are many eye-witness accounts of the prodigious drinking bouts, which pirates used to indulge in. One of the most colourful came from Nathaniel Uring, a merchant sea captain from Norfolk. In 1720 his vessel, the *Bangor Galley*, was shipwrecked in the Bay of Honduras and he was stranded there for five months. He took shelter at the Barcadares, a favourite haunt of pirates and ex-sailors, whom Uring regarded as a 'crew of ungovernable wretches'. He was particularly appalled by their endless drinking sessions, noting in his journal that 'Their chief Delight is in drinking; and when they broach a Hogshead of Wine, they seldom stir from it while there is a Drop left...keeping at it sometimes a Week together, drinking till they fall asleep; and as soon as they awake, at it again...They paid me a considerable Deference,...but I should have been much more agreeable to 'em, if I would have kept 'em Company at their drinking Bouts'.

PIRATES AND POPULAR CULTURE

FOR THOSE WHO did not care to risk their lives on the high seas, the terrible deeds of pirates and buccaneers always held a morbid fascination. While they were alive, their crimes were sensationalised in newspaper reports. Then, once they were dead, they became the subject of lurid ballads and colourful legends. From the outset, it was Blackbeard who attracted the most attention. There were stories about his severed head, which was initially displayed on Lieutenant Maynard's sloop and was subsequently placed on a pole, on the banks of the Hampton River. Rumour had it that the skull was later plated with silver and turned into a punch-bowl by a local tavern-keeper. Unlikely tales about the pirate's headless ghost and his hidden treasure were also widely circulated.

Blackbeard's exploits soon became the inspiration for playwrights and theatre impresarios. In 1798, James Cross produced a 'grand spectacle' entitled *Blackbeard, or the Captive Princess*, which was based very loosely on the pirate's final campaign. One contemporary source described it as 'a serio-comic ballet of action, in two acts', complete with rousing songs, slave dances, cannon fire, and impressive stage effects. The plot revolves around a beautiful Mogul princess and her lover, who are abducted by Blackbeard. The pirate intends to ravish the maid, but is thwarted by the ghost of his wife. In the final scene, Lieutenant Maynard and the Navy arrive to save the day, much to the delight of the audience. The play ran for a season at the Royal Circus in Lambeth, and was revived frequently during the 19th century, largely because of the patriotic flavour of the finale.

As the threat from real pirates began to recede, writers and artists began to glamorise their crimes. The trendsetter in this field was Lord Byron (1788-1824), whose narrative poem, *The Corsair*, caused a sensation, when it was published in 1814. Readers were drawn to its dashing but flawed hero, Conrad the pirate chief. In spite of his cruel past, he displayed great courage in fighting the Turks and saving a slave-girl from a harem. There were rumours that Byron had based the character on himself, and that he had been involved in some form of piracy during his extensive travels. The author laughed off the suggestions, but enjoyed the speculation, which added to his raffish image. The success of the poem inspired a series of works on similar themes. Verdi produced an opera (*Il Corsaro*, 1848) with a libretto based on Byron's piece, while in 1844 Berlioz composed an overture called *Le Corsaire*.

Of course, the taste for pirate material was not confined to the realms of high art; it was equally popular in the most ephemeral, literary forms. The Pirate King became a staple character in creaky melodramas and in the scenarios produced for toy theatres, while penny dreadfuls concentrated on the more lurid end of the market. The latter were sensational stories, which were marketed as serials, selling for a penny a time. They were popular in Britain from the 1830s and, from the outset, pirates were a favourite theme. The most successful of these publications was probably *The Black Pirate, or The Phantom Ship* by William Emans. This first appeared in 1838 and was reissued a decade later in 36 parts. Other bestsellers

included *The Death Ship, or The Pirate's Bride and the Maniac of the Deep* (32 parts, 1846); *The Corsair, or The Foundling of the Sea* (6 parts, 1847); and *Black Rollo, the Pirate, or The Dark Woman of the Deep* (93 parts, 1866).

Gilbert and Sullivan were deeply influenced by this kind of material. The full title of their pirate work - *The Pirates of Penzance, or The Slave of Duty* (1879) - reads like the name of a penny dreadful, while their Pirate King is a lively parody of the villains of Victorian melodramas. In fact, Gilbert had some personal experience of brigandage - as a boy, he had been kidnapped in Naples by a very polite bandit - and the pair suffered from a different form of piracy. Their work was invariably pirated in the US, and this led them to take extraordinary measures with *Pirates*. The work could only be protected, if it was premiered in Britain and the US at virtually the same time. As a result, the very first performance was staged by a touring cast of *H.M.S. Pinafore*, in the unlikely venue of the Royal Bijou Theatre in Paignton. The players wore pirate bandanas over their *Pinafore* costumes and, immediately after the show, the libretto and orchestral parts were locked away.

The jovial rogues in *The Pirates of Penzance* bore no relation to any real-life pirates. In the piece, they turn out to be 'noblemen gone wrong' and are easily reformed. However, these amiable caricatures have had a significant influence on the public view of piracy, simply because the operetta is still so widely performed.

Although the legacy of Byron, Scott, and Gilbert and Sullivan is important, the lasting popularity of pirate themes owes more to the emergence of children's literature. The earliest books in this field often laid a heavy emphasis on morality and instruction but, by the mid-

19th century, there was a growing demand for pure, escapist entertainment. Lively adventure stories were particularly popular and, from the 1840s, these increasingly featured pirates and buccaneers. Harriet Martineau's *Feats on the Fjord* (1841) and W.H.G. Kingston's *Peter the Whaler* (1851) were two of the first examples and the trend reached a peak with Robert Louis Stevenson's *Treasure Island* (1882).

Stevenson got the idea for his groundbreaking pirate book during a family holiday in Braemar in 1881. Spurred on by an initial burst of enthusiasm, he wrote the first half of the story very quickly, at the rate of a chapter a day. After this, he ran out of inspiration and might easily have abandoned the project, if he had not received an offer to serialise the tale in a magazine called *Young Folks*. With this in mind, Stevenson finished the story in early 1882, while staying at Davos in Switzerland. At the suggestion of the editor, James Henderson, Stevenson changed its title from *The Sea Cook* to *Treasure Island*.

The story was serialised in 18 parts, appearing under a suitably nautical pseudonym, Captain George North. It received a moderate reception, but did well enough to gain the author a book deal. Stevenson was offered £100 for the rights and accepted gleefully, writing to his parents 'A hundred pounds, all alive, oh! A hundred jingling, tingling, golden, minted quid. Is not this wonderful?'

Stevenson used a wide variety of sources for *Treasure Island*. He cited, in particular, *The Gold Bug* (1843) by Edgar Allan Poe, which was about the legendary buried treasure of Captain Kidd. The island itself appears to have been based on California, where Stevenson had spent his honeymoon in 1880. The author himself described the setting more enigmatically as 'Californian in part, and in part *chic*'.

After Long John Silver, the most famous fictional pirate is the villainous Captain Hook, in *Peter Pan* (1904). The author, J.M. Barrie (1860-1937) had been fascinated by pirates ever since childhood. As a youngster, he had played 'pirates and redskins' with his chums; had loved penny dreadfuls, such as *Dare Devil Dick*; and had read adventure stories, such as *The Coral Island* (1858) by R.M. Ballantyne (1825-94). Even as an adult, when he was playing with the Davies children, Barrie would pretend to be a wicked pirate, Captain Swarthy.

Hook was probably a combination of several characters, remembered from his childhood. In part, he was inspired by Hooky Crewe, a postman at Thrums, who had lost his right hand and replaced it with an iron hook. The more malicious aspects of Hook's character came from a hated master at his school. Barrie was certainly conscious of this as, in one of his drafts of *Peter Pan*, the pirate escaped from the crocodile and became a schoolmaster. In addition, there are echoes of Long John Silver. Both had a disability, which they could turn to their advantage - Silver's crutch was as deadly a weapon as the captain's hook.

The names of Hook's followers were either based on the author's friends, or on genuine pirates. Canary Robb, for example, was inspired by James Robb, one of Barrie's childhood playmates. On the other hand, Mullins, Cookson, and Murphy were all authentic pirate names. Darby Mullins, for instance, ran a punch house for buccaneers in Jamaica, before joining up with William Kidd's crew and getting himself hanged, along with his captain.

The role was created by Gerald du Maurier, the uncle of Peter Llewelyn Davies, Barrie's model for Peter Pan. The list refers only to initial appearances in the role. Some actors - notably Alastair Sim and Ron Moody - played Hook in several productions.

One of the great unsung heroes of pirate culture is the American author-illustrator, Howard Pyle (1853-1911). He produced a wide variety of children's stories, but had a particular fascination for pirates. After his death, his stories and illustrations on this theme were collected into a single volume, *Howard Pyle's Book of Pirates* (1921). The stories may have dated a little, but the illustrations remain highly influential and have done much to shape the public perception of pirates, appearing in virtually every book on the subject. One of Pyle's pupils, N.C. Wyeth (1882-1945), produced illustrations for the 1911 edition of *Treasure Island*.

Pirate subjects had an obvious appeal for Hollywood, with their winning combination of action, romance, and exotic locations. Several films were made during the silent era, including early versions of *Treasure Island* (1920) and *Peter Pan* (1924), *The Sea Hawk* (1924), *Captain Blood* (1925), and - best of all - *The Black Pirate* (1926), featuring Douglas Fairbanks Senior in one of his most dashing roles.

With the arrival of sound, pirate films became the preserve of the matinee idol. Errol Flynn starred in two of the better examples, the remakes of *Captain Blood* (1935) and *The Sea Hawk* (1940); Tyrone Power sparkled in *The Black Swan* (1942), which was loosely based on the life of Henry Morgan; while Burt Lancaster used his training as a circus acrobat to good effect in *The Crimson Pirate* (1952).

None of these films made any pretence of presenting an accurate picture of pirate life. They were meant as

ACTORS WHO HAVE PLAYED CAPTAIN HOOK

Over the years, an amazing variety of performers have tackled this famous pirate part, ranging from Shakespearean actors and Hollywood icons to stand-up comedians and soap stars.

Gerald du Maurier
1904-05 *Duke of York's Theatre, London*

Leslie Banks
1924 *Knickerbocker Theater, New York*

Ralph Richardson
1933-34 *Palladium, London*

Charles Laughton
1936-37 *Palladium, London*

Seymour Hicks
1938-39 *Palladium, London*

Alastair Sim
1941-42 *Adelphi Theatre, London*

Boris Karloff
1950 *Imperial Theater, New York*

Donald Wolfit
1953-54 *Scala Theatre, London*

Stanley Holloway
1954 *Touring company*

Donald Sinden
1960-61 *Scala Theatre, London*

John Gregson
1961-62 *Scala Theatre, London*

Ron Moody
1966-67 *Scala Theatre, London*

Eric Porter
1971-72 *Coliseum, London*

Dave Allen
1973-74 *Coliseum, London*

Joss Ackland
1982-83 *Barbican, London*

George Cole
1986-87 *Drury Lane Theatre Royal, London*

Leslie Grantham
1999-2000 *Wimbledon Theatre, London*

rousing, escapist entertainment and succeeded admirably on that level. Nevertheless, they helped to promote the image of pirates as bold adventurers or renegades. The violence and cruelty of the real buccaneers was deliberately played down. The movies were equally misleading in another, less obvious manner. They gave the impression that pirates always sailed in huge ships. There was a practical reason for this. Even though the action scenes aboard ship were generally filmed in studio tanks, rather than at sea, the actors needed plenty of room to display their dazzling swordplay and athletic stunts, such as swinging through the rigging. In reality, most pirates operated in small sloops, so their fights generally took place in rather cramped conditions.

Many actors have portrayed pirates as swashbuckling adventurers, but very few have captured their more sinister side. The glorious exception is Robert Newton (1905-

56), whose scurrilous leer and rich, west-country accent have come to epitomise many people's idea of a real pirate. Newton played the title role in *Blackbeard the Pirate* (1952), but is best known for his definitive performance as Long John Silver in *Treasure Island* (1950). This proved so successful that he reprised the role in an Australian film (*Long John Silver*, 1953) and in a television series (*The Adventures of Long John Silver*, 1957), which was completed shortly before his death.

Newton was born in Shaftesbury, in Dorset, and went to school in Cornwall. He drew on these west-country roots when he developed his distinctive pirate brogue, which proved an inspiration both for the *Pirates of the Caribbean* films and 'Talk like a Pirate Day'.

For many years, the cartoon adventures of *Captain Pugwash* provided a comic slant on pirate activities. The eponymous hero was the podgy skipper of the *Black Pig* who, together with his work-shy crew, spent most of his time trying to avoid the murderous clutches of Cut Throat Jake. This long-running children's show was first televised in the 1950s (1957-66) and was later revived in a colour series (1974-75). It was written and drawn by John Ryan. Although *Captain Pugwash* is best known as a television show, the character was first seen in a comic-strip in the *Eagle* (1950).

The Buccaneers (1956-57) was a short-lived, but highly popular television series. It starred Robert Shaw as Dan Tempest, a former pirate leader who had taken the king's pardon in 1718 and was now helping to defend the colonies in the Bahamas. Tempest had a pet monkey called Captain Morgan, while his action scenes were filmed on the same ship that had featured in Disney's *Treasure Island*.

Several rock bands have used pirate accessories to add colour to their act, but none took it to quite the same extremes as Johnny Kidd and the Pirates. Kidd, whose real name was Frederick Heath, started out playing skiffle in a group called Freddie and the Nutters, but changed his image entirely when he switched to rock 'n' roll. In addition to the pirate name, he donned an eyepatch, wielded a cutlass, and played against a backdrop of a galleon. The group achieved a no.1 hit with 'Shakin' All Over', but Heath's career was cut tragically short, when he was killed in a car crash in 1966.

A different type of pirate took to the waves in 1964. On Easter Sunday, Radio Caroline, the first of the pirate radio ships, began broadcasting. The scheme was the brainchild of an Irish businessman, Rohan O'Rahilly. He converted an old trawler into a floating radio station, in a bid to break the BBC's monopoly of sound broadcasting. A second station, Radio London, was launched in December and, by 1967, no fewer than nine new outfits were operating off the coast of Britain.

The pirates proved an immediate success, capturing a youth market that the BBC had neglected. The government eventually blocked these activities through the Marine Broadcasting (Offences) Act (1967), although not before the BBC had been prompted to change its service, creating Radio 1. In spite of their popularity, the pirates were true to the spirit of their namesakes - they usurped their own frequencies, paid no royalties, and took little notice of copyright or performance laws.

If *Treasure Island* and *Peter Pan* did much to create the earliest popular image of pirates, then the biggest influence today is the trilogy of *Pirates of the Caribbean* movies. Uniquely, these films did not draw their initial inspiration from a book, a play, or a picture. Instead, they evolved out of a ground-breaking ride in a theme park. Ever since it was opened, on March 18, 1967, the *Pirates of the Caribbean* ride has been one of the main attractions at Disneyland. Variations of it were installed in the Magic Kingdom at Walt Disney World (1973), Tokyo Disneyland (1983), and Disneyland Paris (1992).

The attraction was originally conceived in the 1950s as a type of wax museum, where visitors could walk through a number of static scenes. The project was transformed, however, after Disney became involved in the 1964 World's Fair in New York. He was particularly impressed with the boat rides, which had proved so popular at the fair, and was anxious to adapt his pirate attraction into a similar format. He also pioneered the use of 'audio-animatronics' (a combination of sound, anima-

SPORTS TEAMS WITH PIRATE NAMES

Amsterdam Pirates	Dutch Baseball
Blackburn Rovers	English Football
Bristol Rovers	English Football
Canberra Raiders	Australian Rugby League
Cornish Pirates	English Rugby Union
Oakland Raiders	American Football
Orlando Pirates	South African Football
Pittsburgh Pirates	American Baseball
Portland Pirates	American Hockey
Tampa Bay Buccaneers	American Football
Tampa Bay Mutiny	American Soccer

tion, and electronics), which enabled his technicians to produce lifelike, moving pirates.

The original ride drew some of its elements from the film, *Treasure Island* (1950), which had been Disney's first live action film. In its turn, the first *Pirates of the Caribbean* movie borrowed several details from the ride, including the talking skeletons, the cursed treasure, and the pirate attack on a fortress. Fittingly, the world premiere of *Pirates of the Caribbean* was an open-air screening at Disneyland.

The key to the phenomenal success of *Pirates of the Caribbean* was Johnny Depp's swaggering performance as Captain Jack Sparrow. The actor based his performance on a surprising combination of sources. When he was first offered the role, he tried to imagine the nearest, modern equivalent to swashbuckling pirates and decided that the answer was probably rock stars. So he approached his friend, Keith Richards of the Rolling Stones, and asked if he could model some elements of Sparrow on him. Bizarrely, Depp also drew inspiration from a cartoon character - Pepe Le Pew, an amorous skunk.

Depp went to considerable lengths to ensure that his pirate seemed authentic. He made exhaustive attempts to perfect a rolling, seaman's gait, even practising the walk off set, and he spent a lot of time in his sauna, to gauge the effects of the sweltering, Caribbean climate. He also had several teeth capped with gold, and wore a temporary tattoo of a sparrow on his right arm. Depp later replaced this with a permanent tattoo, adding his son's name - 'Jack'.

The villain in the first *Pirates of the Caribbean* film was Barbossa, played by Geoffrey Rush. In name, at least, this character evoked the memory of two genuine pirates. The

Barbarossa (literally 'Red Beard') brothers were Turkish corsairs, operating in the Mediterranean in the early sixteenth century. One of them, Kheir-ed-Din became the Regent of Algiers in 1530.

Barbossa was almost upstaged by his pet monkey, which he called Jack - as a slighting reference to Jack Sparrow. The part was 'acted' by Tara and Levi, the two capuchin monkeys who took turns in playing the role. Their trainers had no trouble in assisting with the action sequences. Ironically, the most difficult task was to persuade them to sit still, during the scenes with dialogue. They solved the problem by squirting a little water on the monkeys' jackets, prior to each of these scenes. This distracted the creatures momentarily, just long enough for the actor to hurriedly speak his lines.

When Blackbeard, Black Bart, and Captain Kidd were wreaking havoc on the high seas, they could never have imagined that, in the future, pirates would have a special day dedicated to their memory. In 1995, 'International Talk like a Pirate Day' was introduced as a private joke by two Americans, John Baur ('Ol' Chum Bucket') and Mark Summers ('Cap'n Slappy'). Summers chose September 19 as the day in question, as it was his ex-wife's birthday, so he knew he would find it easy to remember. To their surprise, the idea caught on and it is now used as a means of raising funds for charitable causes. Participants are sponsored to go into school or work dressed as a pirate, or to keep up a pirate accent for the whole day. So, against all the odds, pirates are now involved in charity work.

TO THE
HESITATING PURCHASER

If sailor tales to sailor tunes,
Storm and adventure, heat and cold,
If schooners, islands, and maroons
And Buccaneers and buried Gold,
And all the old romance, retold
Exactly in the ancient way,
Can please, as me they pleased of old,
The wiser youngsters of to-day:

- So be it, and fall on! If not,
If studious youth no longer crave,
His ancient appetites forgot,
Kingston*, or Ballantyne* the brave,
Or Cooper* of the wood and wave;
So be it, also! And may I
And all my pirates share the grave
Where these and their creations lie!

*authors of children's adventure stories

BIBLIOGRAPHY

Black, Clinton V. *Pirates of the West Indies*, Cambridge University Press,1989

Botting, Douglas *The Pirates*, Time-Life Books Inc., 1978

Carpenter, Humphrey and **Prichard, Mari** *The Oxford Companion to Children's Literature*, OUP, 1984

Cordingly, David *Life Among the Pirates, The Romance and the Reality*, Little, Brown and Company, 1995

Earle, Peter *The Pirate Wars*, Methuen Publishing Ltd., 2003

Green, Roger Lancelyn *Fifty Years of Peter Pan*, Peter Davies, 1954

Lane, Kris *Blood and Silver, A History of Piracy in the Caribbean and Central America*, Signal Books Ltd., 1999

Mitchell, David *Pirates*, Thames and Hudson, 1976

Parry, Dan *Blackbeard, The Real Pirate of the Caribbean*, National Maritime Museum Publishing, 2006

Skowronek, Russell and Ewen, Charles *X Marks the Spot, The Archaeology of Piracy*, University Press of Florida, 2006

Souhami, Diana *Selkirk's Island*, Weidenfeld & Nicolson, 2001

Starkey, David ed. *Pirates and Privateers*, University of Exeter Press, 1997

Stevenson, Robert Louis *Treasure Island*, Cassell, 1883

Zacks, Richard *The Pirate Hunter, The True Story of Captain Kidd*, Hyperion, 2002

Useful Websites

www.piratesinfo.com/main.php - Pirates: Fact and Legend

www.geocities.com/captcutlass/ - Brethren of the Coast; Buccaneers

www.talklikeapirate.com/piratehome.html - Talk like a Pirate Day

www.whydah.com/ - Whydah expedition

blindkat.hegewisch.net/pirates/pirates.html - Pirates of the Caribbean, Fact and Fiction

www.noquartergiven.net/ - Pirate magazine. Festivals

www.bonaventure.org.uk/ed/piratemythtory.htm - Pirate legends

www.mooncove.com/newton/index.htm - Robert Newton site

www.cindyvallar.com/pirates.html - Pirates and Privateers

www.thepiratesrealm.com/ - Pirate history and information

www.coinsite.com/ - Pirate coins

www.kipar.org/piratical-resources/pirate-history.html - History Resources for Pirates of the Caribbean